Editor
Tracy Edmunds

Managing Editors
Karen J. Goldfluss, M.S. Ed.
Ina Massler Levin, M.A.

Cover Artist
Marilyn Goldberg

Art Production Manager
Kevin Barnes

Imaging
Rosa C. See

Publisher
Mary D. Smith, M.S. Ed.

Writing and Reading Mysteries

Grades 4–8

Author

Helen Hoffner, Ed.D.

Teacher Created Resources, Inc.
6421 Industry Way
Westminster, CA 92683
www.teachercreated.com
ISBN-1-4206-3609-x

©2006 Teacher Created Resources, Inc.
Made in U.S.A.

The classroom teacher may reproduce copies of materials in this book for classroom use only. The reproduction of any part for an entire school or school system is strictly prohibited. No part of this publication may be transmitted, stored, or recorded in any form without written permission from the publisher.

Table of Contents

Introduction 3
Mysteries at Home
    Hometown Mysteries 4
    Investigating Change 8
Mysteries in History
    Mysteries in History 10
    Writing Historical Mysteries 14
Clues and Cues
    Scales of Justice 17
    Want-Ad Mysteries 19
    Secret Codes 20
    Secret Code 22
    Identifying the Suspects 23
    Round Up the Suspects 25
    Mystery Hunt 27
Skills and Strategies
    Convince Me! 29
    Syllogism Sleuths 30
    Sorting It Out 33
    Unlocking Words 36
    Strange Sounding Words 39
Making Predictions
    Perplexing Predictions 41
    Clozing the Case 44
Mysteries and Poetry
    Mystery for Two Voices 46
    Puzzling Poems 48
Literature Based Mysteries
    What's Up, Sherlock? Learning About Sherlock Holmes ... 49
    The Power of Observation 52
    The Eleventh Hour: Time to Start a Mystery 53
    The Mysteries of Harris Burdick 54
    Drawing a Mystery 56
    The Mystery Picture Party 57
    Two Sides to Every Story 60
    Mystery Reviews 61
Mysterious Oral Reading
    Shivering Mystery Theater 63
    Back Cover Voices 66
The Mystery Series
    The Mystery Series 67
    Favorite Mystery Series 68
    A New Adventure Starring My Favorite Detective 70
    Another Exciting Episode: Mystery Series to Explore . 72
Mysteries Too Good to Miss 75
Resources for Mystery Lovers 77

Introduction

Mysteries are everywhere. A friend's secretive behavior, an unexpected change in neighborhood traffic patterns, or the closing of a favorite store may compel us to ask questions and seek solutions. Although we often find mysteries close to home, we also wonder at the seemingly mysterious events we read about in history books. The 1947 appearance of Unidentified Flying Objects (UFO's) in Roswell, New Mexico, the building of the Stonehenge Monument in southwestern England, and the disappearance of Amelia Earhart are among the great unsolved mysteries of history. Mysteries large and small challenge us to make predictions, gather clues, and support our suspicions with evidence.

Teachers can reinforce vital literacy skills and strategies by introducing students to the mystery genre. When students read and write mysteries, they have opportunities to form and test hypotheses, evaluate clues, and conduct research. *Writing and Reading Mysteries* enables teachers and students to meet curriculum standards while reading and writing intriguing tales.

Writing and Reading Mysteries in Grades contains lesson plans, worksheets, and book lists which can be used to enhance literacy instruction while students read any mystery novel or short story. There are activities for whole-class, small group, and individualized instruction. The text is divided into sections to help teachers quickly find appropriate activities and worksheets. The initial sections include:

- *Mysteries at Home*
- *Mysteries in History*
- *Clues and Cues*
- *Skills and Strategies*
- *Making Predictions*
- *Mysteries and Poetry*
- *Literature Based Mysteries*
- *Mysterious Oral Reading*

The Mystery Series section, discusses classic mystery series, such as the *Nancy Drew Mysteries* and the *Hardy Boys Mysteries*, as well as modern popular mystery series, including the *Sammy Keyes* series and the *A to Z Mysteries*. Also included are annotated lists of classic mystery series, recently published mystery series, and mystery series for students in grades 4 to 7 who may be reading below their grade level. The final section lists great mysteries for students ages 9 to 12.

McREL (Mid-continent Research for Education and Learning) standards and benchmarks are given for each lesson. These standards and benchmarks can be found at the McREL website: www.mcrel.org/standards-benchmarks

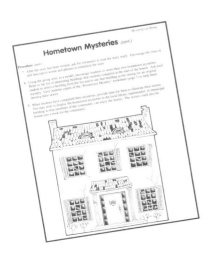
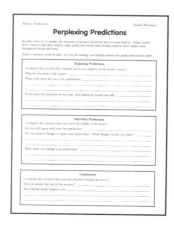

Mysteries at Home

Hometown Mysteries

In every town there is an old building with a legend attached. Perhaps it is the forgotten railroad station with dusty windows and empty ticket counters. It could be the abandoned school where rusting cars and scrap metal fill the deserted playground. The town may hold a house where weeds have grown high and the glass windows have been shattered. These landmarks can inspire your students to read and write mysteries.

> **Objective:** Students will write a mystery using a building in their hometown as the setting.
>
> **Standard:** Uses the general skills and strategies of the writing process
>
> **Benchmark:** Writes narrative accounts, such as poems and stories
>
> **Skill Development:** Interviewing, forming inferences, writing skills
>
> **Organization:** Whole-class activity, pairs, and independent work

Materials

- overhead transparencies of "Sample Hometown Mystery" (page 6) and "Hometown Mystery" worksheet (page 7)
- student copies of the "Hometown Mystery" worksheet (page 7)
- chalkboard and chalk, dry erase board and markers, or chart paper and markers

Procedure

1. Initiate a discussion of special buildings in your town. Do you have an historic police station, library, or railroad station? Is your town the birthplace of an author, president, or sports star? Are there unique schools or churches in your town? Ask students to name interesting buildings in your town. Write their suggestions on the chalkboard or dry erase board.

2. Ask students if they are aware of any stories about the unique buildings in their town. Provide time for students to tell stories about the buildings.

3. Select one building from the students' list that seems to have an interesting past and seems to be associated with many stories. Invite students to work as a whole class to write a mystery with that special building as the setting.

4. Read aloud the "Sample Hometown Mystery" (page 6) to give students an idea of how to create a mystery. You may wish to make an overhead transparency of this sample worksheet so students can read along.

5. Using an overhead transparency of the "Hometown Mystery" worksheet (page 7), have students discuss a story idea as a group. Help the students answer the questions and develop a plot.

6. Using chart paper, a chalkboard, or dry erase board, invite the class to write the mystery as a group. Students can dictate sentences or can take turns writing them.

Hometown Mysteries (cont.)

Procedure (cont.)

7. After the story has been written, ask for volunteers to read the story orally. Encourage the class to add descriptive words and phrases to embellish the story.

8. Using the group story as a model, encourage students to write their own hometown mysteries. Refer to the list of interesting buildings that students compiled at the start of the lesson. Ask each student to select a building from the list and to use that building as the setting for an original mystery. Give students copies of the "Hometown Mystery" worksheet (page 7) to help them develop their stories.

9. When students have completed their mysteries, provide time for them to illustrate their stories. You may wish to display the hometown mysteries in the local library, supermarket, or municipal building so that members of the community can enjoy the stories. The stories could also be bound into a book for the community.

Sample Hometown Mystery

1. What is the setting for your mystery? Give a name for the building and state the date or time period in which the mystery occurred.

    The old Ridley Park Train Station, August 1946

2. What makes this building unusual or interesting? (For example, the building might have a balcony, secret staircase, or a basement swimming pool.)

    Unlike most train stations, the Ridley Park Train Station has a small free library next to the ticket counter. Before boarding a train, passengers may select books from the shelf. The passengers can read the books as they wait in the station or they can take the books with them to read as they ride on the trains.

3. What special event or mystery took place in that building?

    When commuters picked up books, they noticed that someone had been leaving notes in the books. One note said, "There is an envelope with money hidden behind the water fountain." When the commuter looked, he found an envelope containing $50.00. Other notes told commuters where they could find valuable jewelry and autographed books hidden in the train station.

4. What is the main idea of the mystery you will write?

    Three students follow clues to learn why someone hid money and valuable objects in the train station for commuters to find.

5. Name three main characters and give a brief description of each character. Example:

Character	Description
Claude Alpern	— Ridley Park Trainmaster — Enjoys reading — Enjoys talking to the commuters each day
Martha Simon	— Lives in Ridley Park and rides the train to her job in a school in Philadelphia each day — Likes to read — Constantly asking questions of the other commuters — Constantly snooping in every corner of the train station
Mary Connors	— Sits quietly in the train station every day — Rides the train to her job at a bank in Philadelphia — Always carries a large shopping bag

Mysteries at Home   Student Worksheet

Hometown Mystery

You don't have to go far to discover a mystery. Mysteries can be found in your own hometown!

1. Select an interesting building in your town. Have you heard any unusual stories about that building? Have any special events been held in that building? Have any famous people lived there?
2. Think about the old stories you may have heard about that building. You can exaggerate or embellish those old stories to write your own mystery. If you have not heard any stories about the interesting building you selected, then it is time for you to create a tale.
3. Use the questions below to plan your story.
4. After answering the questions, use your answers to write a draft of your mystery.
5. Read your draft to a classmate. Use your classmate's comments to revise your story and make it even better.
6. Complete a final draft of your mystery.

Answer the questions below to create a hometown mystery.

1. What is the setting for your mystery? Give a name for the building and state the date or time period in which the mystery occurred.

   _____

   _____

2. What makes this building unusual or interesting?

   _____

   _____

3. What special event or mystery took place in that building?

   _____

   _____

4. What is the main idea of the mystery you will write?

   _____

   _____

5. Use the table below to name three main characters and give a brief description of each character.

Character	Description

© Teacher Created Resources, Inc.

Mysteries at Home

Investigating Change

Change can be frustrating and cause tempers to flare. Residents often become angry when there are changes in traditional events or policies in a community. When citizens learn the reasons for a change, however, they are often more accepting and supportive of new ideas.

Help your students understand changes in their community by inviting them to investigate the reasons for a change.

Objectives: Students will interview local leaders and read newspaper reports to learn why a change has taken place in their community.

Students will give an oral presentation for their classmates.

Standard: Gathers and uses information for research purposes

Benchmark: Uses strategies to gather and record information for research topics

Standard: Uses listening and speaking strategies for different purposes

Benchmark: Makes basic oral presentations to class

Skill Development: Research techniques, speaking and listening skills

Organization: Whole-class activity, small groups

Materials
- copies of "Investigating Change" worksheet and rubric (page 9) for each group

Procedure

1. Ask your students to list changes that have occurred recently in their community. Examples: Are there new restrictions on swimming, boating, or fishing in the lake? Has the community instituted a new curfew for young people? Has the community prohibited skateboarding in the park? Are owners now required to keep their dogs on a leash when walking in the park?

2. Ask the students to form groups with four to six members. Ask each group to discuss one of the changes that has recently taken place in the community.

3. Give each group the task of investigating the reasons for a change. The students can search the Internet, view local television stations, read the local newspaper, and contact community leaders. Distribute the "Investigating Change" worksheet and rubric (page 9) to help students organize their work.

4. After learning the reasons for a change, each group should prepare a presentation for their classmates. In their presentation, students must show evidence that they have found the true reason for the change in their community. Like good detectives, students must prove that they have found a credible source of information. Remind them to look over the rubric, as it will be used to evaluate their presentations.

5. Schedule presentation for the class. Use the rubric (page 9) to evaluate the group presentations.

Mysteries at Home   *Student Worksheet*

Investigating Change

Group Members: _____

_____

_____

The change in our community that we have investigated is: _____

_____

_____

To investigate this change we interviewed: _____

_____

We read reports about this change in: (List newspapers, magazines, and Internet sources.)

_____

_____

After learning the facts, we feel that this change was (good/bad) for the community because

_____

_____

_____

_____

Rubric for Evaluating the Presentation

	Possible	Your Points	Comments
Collaboration: Did everyone work together to investigate the change? Did everyone participate equally in the presentation?	25		
Did the group list reliable sources for their information?	25		
Did group members speak clearly during the presentation?	25		
Did the group hold the attention of the audience?	25		
Total Score	100		

Mysteries in History

Mysteries in History

Did an alien spaceship land in Roswell, New Mexico? What happened to Amelia Earhart? Who created the stone columns at Stonehenge? Is there a monster in Loch Ness? These mysteries have confounded historians and scientists for many years. Invite your students to learn more about history's unsolved mysteries by conducting their own research. A study of these mysteries can help your students develop research and reporting skills, as well as an appreciation for the work of scientists and historians.

> **Objective:** Students will compose a one-page report and give a five-minute oral presentation on an unsolved historical mystery.
>
> **Standard:** Gathers and uses information for research purposes
>
> **Benchmarks:** Uses a variety of resource material to gather information for research topics
>
> Determines the appropriateness of an information source for a research topic
>
> Writes research papers
>
> **Standard:** Uses listening and speaking strategies for different purposes
>
> **Benchmarks:** Plays a variety of roles in group discussion
>
> Makes oral presentations to the class
>
> **Skill Development:** Locating and evaluating resource materials
>
> **Organization:** Whole-class activity and small group

Materials

- access to the Internet
- access to a school or community library
- one copy of the "Mysteries in History" group assignment chart (page 11)
- one copy per group of the "Mysteries in History" assignment and reporting sheet (page 12) and the presentation rubric (page 13)

Procedure

1. Begin by discussing the unsolved historical mystery of the Lost City of Atlantis. Ask students to talk about what they have heard and state their theories about Atlantis. Tell the class that Atlantis is just one of many unsolved historical mysteries.

2. Show students the "Mysteries in History" group assignment chart (page 11) and discuss each of the mysteries.

3. Post the group assignment chart and provide time for the students to sign their names under a topic that they wish to research.

4. Designate sections of the classroom as meeting places for students who have selected the same topic. Distribute the "Mysteries in History" assignment and reporting sheet and the presentation rubric (pages 12–13) to each group. Tell the groups that they are responsible for completing the worksheets and making an oral presentation to the entire class.

5. Provide time for the groups to meet to complete their work.

6. Schedule the presentations for the class. Use the presentation rubric (page 13) to evaluate the group presentations.

Mysteries in History Group Assignment Chart

Mysteries in History

Sign your name under the topic which you wish to investigate.

Loch Ness Monster	Bermuda Triangle	Atlantis	UFOs in Roswell, New Mexico

Amelia Earhart	Stonehenge	Crop Circles

Mysteries in History   *Student Worksheet*

Mysteries in History

Assignment Sheet

Topic: _____

Group Members: _____

1. Begin your research by using a search engine to find information on the Internet related to your topic.
2. Visit three to five websites and print information on your topic.
3. Read the information with members of your group.
4. Visit the school library to find additional information on your topic.
5. Complete the Reporting Sheet below.
6. Prepare a five-minute presentation for the class, using the presentation rubric as a guide. Your group must make a poster to show during the presentation, and your group must compose a one page, typed report about the topic.

Reporting Sheet

1. What did you know about this topic before you started your research?
   _____
   _____

2. What additional information did you learn about this topic?
   _____
   _____

3. What do you think really happened? What is the solution to this mystery?
   _____
   _____

4. List books, magazines, and newspapers used in your research.
   _____
   _____

5. List websites used in your research. _____

Mysteries in History   *Student Worksheet*

Mysteries in History
Presentation Rubric

	Yes/No	Comments
Did the group use at least three websites to find information?		
Did the group prepare a five-minute presentation?		
Did the group prepare a poster for the presentation?		
Did the group compose a one page report?		
Did all members of the group participate in the presentation?		

Mysteries in History

Writing Historical Mysteries

Note: This lesson should take place after the students have completed the preceding Mysteries in History lesson, as students will be working in their groups from that lesson. The Mysteries in History lesson will expose the students to actual historical mysteries that the students can use as models for writing their own mysteries.

As your students explore unsolved historical mysteries, they will learn a great deal about the lifestyles of people who lived long ago. They will understand the ways in which transportation options and obstacles, medical knowledge, dress, and job opportunities of an historical period led to mysteries and speculation.

After investigating an unsolved historical mystery, invite your students to use the information they have gathered to create historical fiction. The students can work independently, in pairs, or in small groups to write a mystery using actual historical characters and events.

Objective: Students will write an historical mystery selection based upon a mystery they have investigated.

Standard: Uses the general skills and strategies of the writing process

Benchmark: Writes narrative accounts, such as short stories

Skill Development: Use of descriptive vocabulary, sentence structure, sequencing, research skills

Organization: Whole-class activity and small group work

Materials

- Historical fiction selections
- Student copies of the "Writing Historical Mysteries" worksheet (page 16)

Procedure

1. Show the class examples of historical fiction such as *Number the Stars* by Lois Lowry, *Titanic Crossing* by Barbara Williams, or *Johnny Tremain* by Esther Forbes. Discuss the ways in which authors research historical events to create historical fiction.

2. Ask your students to meet with the members of their *Mysteries in History* group to discuss the following questions: Where and when did the mystery take place? Who were the main characters involved in the mystery?

3. Working with their groups, challenge the students to create a fictional mystery selection based upon the historical mystery their group investigated.

Writing Historical Mysteries (cont.)

Procedure (cont.)

4. Distribute the "Writing Historical Mysteries" worksheet (page 16). The students can use this worksheet to organize their ideas for an historical mystery.

5. Provide time for the groups to meet to write their mysteries.

6. You may wish to bind the completed mysteries into a book for the classroom library. Students could also read their mysteries to the class at an assembly.

Mysteries in History   *Student Worksheet*

Writing Historical Mysteries

Historical fiction is a type of writing in which an author uses real events and characters from history to create a fictional story. You and the members of your group have investigated a mystery in history. Now it's time for you to become an author. Create your own historical fiction by developing characters and placing them at the center of the historical mystery you investigated. Complete the worksheet below and then begin writing your mystery on another sheet of paper.

Group Members: _____

Historical Mystery Topic: _____

Setting

1. When did the mysterious events take place?

   _____

2. Where did the mysterious events take place?

   _____

Characters

1. List actual historical figures who were involved in this mystery (i.e., Amelia Earhart, presidents or political figures, etc.).

   _____

2. Create two original characters who will appear in your historical fictional mystery. (Give their names, ages, and a brief description.)

   _____

   _____

   _____

   _____

   _____

   _____

   _____

#3609 *Writing and Reading Mysteries*   © *Teacher Created Resources, Inc.*

Clues and Cues

Scales of Justice

The unfortunate circumstance of being in the wrong place at the wrong time can trap someone in a chain of mysterious, sometimes criminal, events. As detectives work to solve mysteries, innocent people may be unjustly accused and face damage to their reputations and livelihood.

Help your students understand the plight of the unjustly accused by examining episodes in popular novels. This activity will spark class discussion on using caution when attempting to solve mysteries, the rights of the accused, and the principle of innocent until proven guilty.

> **Objective:** Students will reflect upon their reading and list the false accusations that were made against a character in a novel.
> **Standard:** Uses reading skills and strategies to understand and interpret a variety of literary texts
> **Benchmark:** Understands elements of character development
> **Skill Development:** Forming inferences
> **Organization:** Whole-class and independent work

Materials
- trade books
- Student copies of the "Scales of Justice" worksheet (page 18)

Procedure
1. Open the lesson with a discussion of news events and prominent figures who may have been unjustly accused of crimes before sufficient evidence was gathered. Ask the students if they have ever been unjustly accused. Perhaps a student was accused of cheating on a test or in a sporting event. Maybe friends accused a student of telling lies or neglecting group work.
2. Encourage the students to share their feelings on the isolation and frustration that false accusations can bring.
3. Discuss novels the class has read in which the characters face false accusations. Examples of novels in which a character is unjustly accused of a crime are given below:

Novel	Author	Accusation
Holes	Louis Sachar	Stanley is accused of stealing a pair of sneakers.
Laugh Till You Cry	Joan Lowery Nixon	Cody Carter is accused of calling in bomb threats to his middle school.
The Witch of Blackbird Pond	Elizabeth George Speare	Sixteen-year-old Kit Tyler is accused of being a witch.
Gathering Blue	Lois Lowry	Women of the village make accusations against Kira so that they can obtain her land.
I'm Not Who You Think I Am	Peg Kehret	Ginger's favorite teacher, Mr. Wren, may lose his job due to false accusations from angry parents.
Tituba of Salem Village	Ann Petry	Tituba, a slave from Barbados, is accused of being a witch during the Salem trials in 1692.

4. After discussing the novels as a class, distribute the "Scales of Justice" worksheet (page 18). Ask the students to complete the worksheet independently. Provide time for the students to share their responses.

Clues and Cues   *Student Worksheet*

Scales of Justice

Has anyone ever said you did something wrong when you really didn't? Did people say you were guilty when you were truly innocent? Sometimes characters in novels are falsely accused of crimes. When we read these novels, we see how false accusations cause tremendous problems for many people, and we also learn how the characters solved their problems and how their friends defended them.

Select a novel in which the main character was falsely accused of a crime. Complete this worksheet and discuss the novel with your classmates.

Novel: _____ Author: _____

Main Character: _____

1. What was the main character accused of? _____
   _____

2. Who made the accusation? _____
   _____

3. Describe the evidence. _____
   _____

4. Did anyone defend the main character? Who? _____
   _____

5. In what ways did the defenders risk their own lives or reputations? _____
   _____

6. Was the main character punished?
   (Examples: Did he or she go to jail or get suspended from school?)
   _____
   _____

7. Was the main character proven innocent? How? _____
   _____

8. Do you think the main character received justice at the conclusion of the novel?
   _____
   _____

Clues and Cues

Want-Ad Mysteries

A quick glimpse of the classified ads in the morning newspaper can give us a peek into our neighbors' lives. We learn of new job openings, businesses for sale, and apartments for rent. The classified ads can also inspire your students to write mysteries.

Objective: Students will write original mysteries based upon newspaper classified advertisements.

Standard: Uses the general skills of the writing process

Benchmark: Writes narrative accounts

Skill Development: Use of descriptive vocabulary, improved sentence structure

Organization: Whole-class activity, independent work

Materials
- the classified advertisements section of the newspaper

Procedure
1. Begin the lesson by reading this actual classified advertisement to your class:

> *Wedding Gown for Sale, Size 10*
> *Ivory Tulle, Beaded Neckline*
> *Veil Included*
> *Never Worn, Asking $400.00*

2. Pose questions such as, "I wonder who is selling the dress. Why do you think the dress was never worn? Did the bride change her mind? Was the wedding cancelled?"

3. Invite the class to suggest reasons to explain why the dress was never worn and why it is now being sold. Provide time for the students to make up stories about the dress.

4. Tell the class that writers can use the classified section of a newspaper to find ideas for stories.

5. Distribute copies of the classified advertisements and ask the students to read and circle interesting items.

6. Encourage each student to select one advertisement to use as the basis for writing a mystery.

7. Monitor the class as they write mysteries inspired by newspaper classified advertisements.

Clues and Cues

Secret Codes

From ancient Egyptian hieroglyphics to today's computer programs, secret codes have been used throughout history to send and receive messages.

Help your students understand the power of communication by introducing them to techniques such as Morse Code, Braille, shorthand, and hieroglyphics.

Objective: Students will conduct research to learn about the development and uses of secret codes.

Standard: Gathers and uses information for research purposes

Benchmark: Uses a variety of resource materials to gather information for research topics

Skill Development: Research skills

Organization: Whole-class activity and small groups

Materials

- group copies of the "Secret Code" worksheet (page 22)
- secret code resources: To conduct this lesson, you will need samples of many types of secret codes. These samples can be found in print sources and through Internet searches. Suggested resources are listed below.

Print Resources

- *The Mysterious Times: Strange Stories of 30 Real-Life Mysteries* by Melissa Heckscher and the Staff of *the Mysterious Times*. This text contains a hieroglyphics alphabet and encourages students to write original messages with hieroglyphics.
- *Writing: A Fact and Fun Book* by Amanda Lewis. *Writing* traces the history of writing from drawings on caves to current publishing trends. There is information on codes such as Braille and hieroglyphics, as well as fascinating trivia concerning the use of codes by historical figures such as Mary, Queen of Scots, and Elizabeth I of England.
- *The Mystery of the Hieroglyphs: The Story of the Rosetta Stone and the Race to Decipher Egyptian Hieroglyphs* by Carol Donoughue. This is a terrific resource for students investigating hieroglyphics. The clear illustrations and helpful glossary make this a reference which students can use independently.

Internet Sources

- Teachers can obtain free Morse Code and Braille samples at the *McType Free Stuff* website: **http://mctype.8m.com/free.things.html**
- Shorthand examples and instructions can be found at the Shorthand, Shorthand, Shorthand website: **http://www.geocities.com/shorthandshorthandshorthand/**
- At the Egyptian hieroglyphs site, teachers will find examples and background information on Egyptian hieroglyphics. This site is student-friendly and could be used directly by students in grades 4 to 7: **http://greatscott.com/hiero**

Secret Codes (cont.)

Related Literature

The use of shorthand figures prominently in the novel *The Shakespeare Stealer* by Gary Blackwood. Students may enjoy reading *The Shakespeare Stealer* as they learn more about shorthand.

Procedure

1. Ask your students to think about the many times during the day when they read and write messages. Then ask your students if they ever use special codes when they write messages. Perhaps they use abbreviations when they take phone messages for family members. Your students might use codes when they send e-mail, text, or instant messages. (Example: LOL means "laugh out loud.")

2. Tell your students that since the earliest days of written language, men and women have been developing special codes to send either abbreviated or secret messages.

3. Show the students samples of codes. Discuss the ways in which codes have been used. Office workers have used shorthand to quickly take notes. Sailors have used Morse Code to communicate with ships at sea. Individuals with visual impairments have used Braille to read texts. Whenever individuals have had a need to communicate, they have developed codes.

4. Divide the students into groups and assign one of the codes, Morse code, Braille, shorthand, or hieroglyphics, to each group. Ask the groups to use reference books and/or the Internet to gather information about their assigned codes.

5. Direct each student to individually write his or her name and one sentence using the secret code assigned to his or her group. (Note: Some codes such as Braille and Morse Code cannot be written with pencil and paper. To replicate these codes, students should make dots for the Braille and Morse Code symbols.)

6. Tell the students to trade sentences with members of their group. Challenge the students to use their knowledge of the secret code to decipher the messages written by their classmates.

7. Ask each group to complete the "Secret Code" worksheet (page 22).

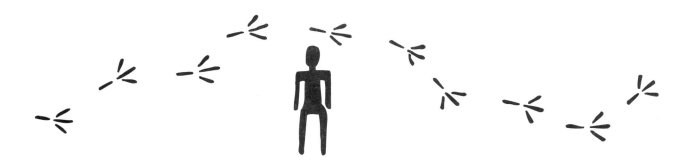

Clues and Cues *Student Worksheet*

Secret Code

Group Members: _____

_____

_____

_____

_____

_____

Our group has been investigating the secret code _____

_____

Our alphabet has 26 letters or symbols. The secret code our group has been studying has _____ symbols.

This secret code was developed by _____

_____

The reason this code was invented was to _____

_____

This secret code has been used to _____

_____

Our group believes that in today's society, this code would be useful to _____

_____

The sentences below have been written in our secret code.

_____

_____

_____

_____

_____

Clues and Cues

Identifying the Suspects

Each of us has physical features and character traits which make us unique. Mystery writers highlight the unique features of their characters to heighten suspense and to show readers the ways in which a fingerprint or strand of hair can reveal someone's identity. This lesson, *Identifying the Suspects*, can help your students recognize their unique characteristics.

Objective: Students will write two to three paragraphs describing their unique personal characteristics.

Standard: Uses the general skills and strategies of the writing process

Benchmark: Writes compositions about autobiographical incidents

Skill Development: Use of descriptive vocabulary, improved sentence structure

Organization: Independent work

Materials

- student copies of the "Identifying the Suspects" worksheet (page 24)
- ink pad for the students to use to make fingerprints
- pictures of the students or crayons and markers for the students to draw pictures of themselves

Procedure

1. After reading a mystery novel, remind your students that detectives often suspect or exonerate a character by examining that character's physical characteristics, such as hair and eye color, as well as his or her habits, such as exercising, shopping at a particular store, or traveling by subway.

2. Ask your students to think about the features which make them unique. Do they have special talents in art, music, or athletics? Do they have long hair or short hair? What color eyes do they have?

3. Encourage your students to think about the features and talents which make them unique. Distribute the "Identifying the Suspect" worksheet (page 24) and ask each student to complete the worksheet.

4. Ask your students to use the information they provided on the worksheet to write two to three paragraphs about themselves.

Clues and Cues   *Student Worksheet*

Identifying the Suspects

Name _____ Date of Birth: _____

Everyone has physical characteristics, such as fingerprints, which make them unique. Detectives identify suspects by their hair color, eye color, and other physical traits. Use the spaces below to record your unique information.

```
┌─────────────────────────────────────────────────────────┐
│                                                         │
│                                                         │
│                                                         │
│                                                         │
│                                                         │
│         Place your photo here or draw a picture         │
│                     of yourself.                        │
├─────────────────────────────────────────────────────────┤
│                                                         │
│                                                         │
│              Place your fingerprints here.              │
└─────────────────────────────────────────────────────────┘
```

Eye color: _____	Height: _____
Hair color: _____	Blood type: _____

In addition to physical traits, everyone has talents or interests which make him or her unique. Think about the characteristics that make you special. Are you an athlete, musician, or writer? What do you like to do after school or on the weekend? Have you ever lived in another state or country? On another sheet of paper, write two to three paragraphs to describe yourself. Include your interests, talents, and goals in your paragraphs

Clues and Cues

Round Up the Suspects

Have any of your students ever lived in another country? Do any of your students have exotic pets? Which of your students has the biggest family? It can be difficult to get to know the background, experiences, talents, and interests of every student in your class. Use the *Round Up the Suspects* lesson to help you and your students learn more about each other.

Objective: Students will question their classmates to learn more about their personal lives.

Standard: Uses listening and speaking strategies for different purposes

Benchmark: Asks questions to seek elaboration and clarification of ideas

Skill Development: Questioning techniques

Organization: Whole class activity

Materials

- student copies of the "Round Up the Suspects" worksheet (page 26)
- kitchen timer

Procedure

1. Begin a class discussion about the experiences and interests which make everyone unique. Maybe you have a student who competes in a sport, such as swimming, gymnastics, or figure skating. Perhaps one of your students has been featured in a newspaper article. Some students have traveled to many states, some have large families, and some have after school jobs which enable them to learn new skills. Tell the class that you will be giving them an opportunity to learn more about each other.

2. Distribute the "Round Up the Suspects" worksheet (page 26). Tell the class that they will have ten minutes to walk around the classroom to try to find at least one classmate who fits each category. Set a kitchen timer to monitor the time for the assignment.

3. Students should spend the allotted ten minutes questioning their classmates so that they can complete the "Round Up the Suspects" worksheet.

4. When the timer rings, ask the students to return to their seats. Share the responses with the entire class.

Clues and Cues *Student Worksheet*

Round Up the Suspects

What do you really know about your classmates? Could they be hiding special talents or secrets? Do they come from big families? Have they lived in exotic places?

Use the table below to learn more about your classmates. Talk to your classmates and try to write at least one name in each row of the table.

Find someone in the class who…

likes to go camping _____

likes to skate _____

likes to swim _____

likes to play soccer _____

has lived on a farm _____

has lived in another country _____

has lived in another state _____

has appeared on television _____

has spoken on the radio _____

has had his or her picture in the newspaper _____

has had his or her name in the newspaper _____

has a dog _____

has a cat _____

has a bird _____

has a goldfish _____

walks to school _____

rides a bike to school _____

rides a bus to school _____

likes to sing _____

likes to dance _____

plays a musical instrument _____

plays on a sports team _____

speaks more than one language _____

has more than two sisters _____

has more than two brothers _____

has a weekend or after school job _____

Clues and Cues

Mystery Hunt

After reading the exploits of detectives such as Nancy Drew and the Boxcar Children, your students may crave their own adventure. Fulfill their wishes by forming teams for a Mystery Hunt!

Objectives: Students will write clues.
Students will read and follow clues.

Standard: Uses the general skills and strategies of the writing process

Benchmark: Uses content, style, and structure appropriate for specific audiences and purposes

Standard: Uses the general skills and strategies of the reading process

Benchmark: Establishes and adjusts purposes for reading

Skill Development: Forming inferences, writing skills, cooperative learning

Organization: small groups

Materials

- paper and pencils
- box to hold final destination slips
- prizes, such as no-homework passes or passes for special privileges such as extra computer time or extra recess

Teacher Preparation

To prepare for the lesson, select final destinations (one for each team), write each final destination on a slip of paper, and place the slips in a box. Then hide prizes at each final destination. Suggested prizes include no-homework passes or tickets for special privileges such as extra recess or computer time. You may wish to limit the mystery hunt to a small area such as one classroom or the playground. Seek approval from the principal and other teachers if the students will be wandering about the entire school.

Procedure

1. Review favorite mysteries the class has read. Discuss the ways in which the characters found clues and followed leads.

2. Tell the class that they will have an opportunity to write clues and to follow clues.

3. Divide the class into teams of three to five members. Ask one member of each team to draw a final destination slip from the box. Remind the teams not to reveal the destinations they have drawn. In order for everyone to enjoy an adventure, there must be secrecy.

Clues and Cues

Mystery Hunt (cont.)

Procedure (cont.)

4. Each team must write five clues to lead other teams to their final destination. Each group should place its clues throughout the school or classroom. You may want to have each group use a different color paper if all groups will be hunting at the same time.

   Examples:

   Clue 1: It's cold in here. I need my jacket!

   (*Clue 2 is hidden in the coat closet.*)

   Clue 2: Now I'm too hot. I need fresh air.

   (*Clue 3 is hidden on the windowsill.*)

   Clue 3: I'm going on a trip and I'll be away for several days. I will leave a message for my teacher and my friends.

   (*Clue 4 is hidden on the ledge of the chalkboard.*)

   Clue 4: It's going to be a long trip. I will take a good book to read on the train.

   (*Clue 5 is hidden in the classroom library.*)

   Clue 5: Now it's time to go. Good-bye everyone!

   (*The final destination is the front door of the classroom. The special prize, an envelope with no-homework passes, is taped to the front door of the classroom.*)

5. Provide time for each team to follow a set of clues to find a prize.

Skills and Strategies

Convince Me!

Detectives and prosecutors use their powers of persuasion to explain mysterious events. Help your students develop confidence in their abilities to use persuasive speaking to state their opinions and win the respect of their peers.

Objective: Students will make persuasive arguments.

Standard: Uses listening and speaking strategies for different purposes

Benchmark: Understands elements of persuasion and appeal in spoken texts

Skill Development: Speaking and listening skills

Organization: Whole-class activity

Materials

None

Procedure

1. Select a situation which requires your students to make a decision that affects the entire class. (Example: Choosing the destination for a field trip)

2. Give the students four options. (Example: Four pre-approved possible destinations for a field trip such as a museum, theater, farm, or factory tour). Tell the class that every student must select one of the four options. Then designate a corner of the room for each option. (Example: Students who want to go to the museum would stand in the right front corner of the classroom, those who want to go to the theater would go to the left front corner of the classroom, etc.). Students should stand in the corner of the room that represents their choice. Some classes will have students standing in all four corners of the classroom. Other classes may have empty corners because no one selected those options.

3. Tell the students that you must reach agreement on this decision and that everyone must be standing in the same corner at the end of the activity. Encourage the students to use persuasive speaking to entice their classmates to leave their respective corners and join their corner. Provide time for students to state their reasons for selecting a particular option.

4. After hearing everyone's reasons, ask if any students have changed their opinions and would like to move to a different corner. Allow students to move to different corners.

5. Continue with the persuasive arguments until the entire class is standing in one corner.

© Teacher Created Resources, Inc.   29   #3609 *Writing and Reading Mysteries*

Skills and Strategies

Syllogism Sleuths

To solve a mystery, readers must use deductive reasoning and evaluate subtle clues. Your students can exercise their powers of deduction when they solve syllogisms—concise arguments with a major and minor premise and a resolution.

Objective: Students will read and solve syllogisms.

Standard: Uses reading skills and strategies to understand and interpret a variety of literary texts

Benchmark: Uses reading skills and strategies to understand a variety of literary passages and texts

Skill Development: Finding clues, reasoning skills

Organization: Whole class activity and pairs

Materials

- copy of the "Syllogism Sleuths" worksheet (page 32) for each pair of students
- chalkboard and chalk, dry erase board and markers, or chart paper and markers

Procedure

1. Tell the class that today they will solve syllogisms, a type of word puzzle. Write the following syllogism on the chalkboard, dry erase board, or chart paper:

   Lightning strikes trees and knocks them down.

   Nicole saw a tree fall during a storm.

   The tree was struck by _____ .

2. Read the syllogism to the class. Guide the students as they solve the syllogism. Fill in the solution.

3. Tell the students that sometimes a reader can be misled. Clues may suggest a simple answer to a mystery. A skilled writer, however, flips the clues and surprises the reader. Write the following syllogism on the board or chart:

   Grandfather clocks chime at midnight.

   Stephen has a grandfather clock.

   Stephen will hear chimes at midnight.

   A reader's first response may be that Stephen heard chimes. There are, however, many other possibilities. Stephen could have been wearing headphones and listening to music at midnight. Stephen could be deaf. Syllogisms help students understand that suspense writers deliberately lead their readers down the wrong paths to create surprising conclusions.

Skills and Strategies

Syllogism Sleuths (cont.)

4. Write the following syllogisms on the board or chart:

   The robber has left a muddy, sneaker footprint.

   Ryan is wearing muddy sneakers.

   Ryan is the robber.

   Old houses have creaky stairs.

   The stairs in the Brady house creak.

   The Brady house is old.

   Discuss the two syllogisms with the class. Are the conclusions accurate? Ask students to come up with alternate conclusions for each syllogism.

5. Ask the students to select a partner. Distribute a copy of the "Syllogism Sleuths" worksheet (page 32) to each pair of students. Each pair of students should discuss the syllogisms on the worksheet and write a response.

6. Provide time for the students to discuss their responses with the entire class.

7. After the students have discussed the syllogisms on the worksheet, invite them to write their own syllogisms based upon the mysteries they are reading.

More Syllogism Examples

Great detectives solve mysteries.

Nancy Drew is a great detective.

Nancy Drew solves mysteries.

Clever children search for clues.

The Boxcar children search for clues.

The Boxcar children are clever.

Skills and Strategies   Student Worksheet

Syllogism Sleuths

Read each syllogism and write a response indicating whether you agree with the conclusion.

1. All police officers enforce their local laws.

    Richard is a police officer.

    Richard enforces the local laws.

    Response: _____

2. All police cars have sirens.

    Gloria's car has a siren.

    Gloria drives a police car.

    Response: _____

3. Jim's math book is missing.

    Tony has two math books.

    Tony has Jim's math book.

    Response: _____

4. The cookie jar was empty.

    Nicole's face was covered with cookie crumbs.

    Nicole took the cookies.

    Response: _____

5. Some thieves tell lies.

    Bill tells lies.

    Bill is a thief.

    Response: _____

6. Brides often wear white dresses.

    Nancy is getting married.

    Nancy will wear a white dress on her wedding day.

    Response: _____

7. Most teachers work in schools.

    Kate is a teacher.

    Kate works in a school.

    Response: _____

8. Spiders build webs.

    Gene found a web in the attic.

    The web was built by a spider.

    Response: _____

Skills and Strategies

Sorting It Out

Good detectives sort through stacks of handwritten notes and newspaper clippings to link clues to a crime. They look for similarities and differences, examine patterns, and find common elements. Your students can participate in similar sorting activities when they categorize and unravel the meaning of unfamiliar words.

Word Sorts is an instructional technique which enables students to group words by features such as spelling patterns, parts of speech, or definition (*Bear et al., 2000*). Encourage your students to build their vocabulary by sorting and discussing the words they will find in mystery novels.

Objectives: Students will sort words into assigned categories.
Students will determine categories to sort words.

Standard: Uses the general skills and strategies of the reading process

Benchmark: Uses a variety of strategies to extend reading vocabulary

Skill Development: Categorizing skills, vocabulary growth

Organization: Whole class and pairs

Materials

- copy of the "Sorting It Out" cards (pages 34–35) for each pair of students
- chalkboard and chalk, dry erase board and markers, or chart paper and markers
- scissors

Procedure

1. Write the words *hero* and *villain* on the chalkboard, dry erase board, or chart paper. Say the words aloud and discuss their meanings with the students. Tell the students that in many mysteries there is a villain who causes bad events to occur and a hero who solves the mystery.

2. Tell the class that they will have an opportunity to learn more words associated with mysteries. Ask each student to find a partner. Give each pair of students one copy of the "Sorting It Out" cards (pages 34–35). Ask each pair to cut the word cards apart.

3. Instruct the students to find the word cards that could be associated with the hero of a mystery (Examples: *police, detective, lawyer*). Then direct the students to find the word cards that might be associated with the villain of a mystery (Examples: *suspect, culprit*).

4. Direct the students to sort the word cards into nouns and verbs. Then, challenge the students to determine their own categories for sorting the words. Your students may suggest categories related to initial consonants, number of syllables, or good and evil characteristics.

Skills and Strategies   *Student Worksheet*

Sorting It Out

Case The detective solved the case.	**Escape** Did the criminal escape from prison?
Conflict There was a conflict between the two detectives who were trying to solve the case.	**Evidence** The detective had evidence to link Jim to the crime.
Clues The detective found new clues at the crime scene.	**Guilty** The evidence proved that Sara was guilty.
Crime The innocent girl did not commit the crime.	**Hero** Ryan became a hero when he rescued the students.
Culprit We knew Tony was the culprit because we found the stolen goods in his pocket.	**Innocent** The evidence proves that Gloria is innocent.
Detective A detective searches for clues and solves crimes.	**Investigate** Officer McCall will investigate and find clues to solve the crime.
Dilemma Our dilemma was that we knew Mary was guilty, but we couldn't prove it.	**Lawyer** My lawyer will prove that I am innocent.

Skills and Strategies

Student Worksheet

Sorting It Out (cont.)

Mystery The detective will solve the mystery.	**Scheme** The criminals tried a new scheme.
Peril The students were in peril when the flood waters rose.	**Suspect** Nicole is a suspect because she was found with the cookies in her hand.
Police The police rescued the stranded motorists.	**Suspense** I am in suspense because I don't know who the winner will be.
Probe The detectives ask many questions when they probe a crime scene.	**Testify** Nancy will testify in court and tell the judge what she saw.
Question The police must question all suspects.	**Victim** I will keep my doors locked so that I don't become a victim of crime.
Rescue Our hero will rescue the cat trapped in the tree.	**Villain** The villain in a novel causes bad events to occur.
Revenge Stephen learned that he should not try to get revenge on the people who testified against him.	

Skills and Strategies

Unlocking Words

Detectives use clues to solve mysteries. Your students can use root words as clues to decipher the meaning of unfamiliar words.

Objective: Students will use root words to determine the meaning of unfamiliar words.

Standard: Uses the general skills and strategies of the reading process

Benchmark: Uses word origins and derivations to understand word meaning (e.g., Latin and Greek roots, meanings of foreign words frequently used in the English language, historical influences on English word meanings)

Skill Development: Determining the meaning of unfamiliar words

Organization: Whole class instruction and independent work

Materials

- chalkboard and chalk, dry erase board and markers, or chart paper and markers
- student copies of the "Unlocking Words" worksheet (pages 37–38)
- dictionary for each student

Procedure

1. Write the word *credible* on the chalkboard, dry erase board, or chart paper. Tell the class that when solving mysteries, law enforcement officials need credible witnesses. Ask students if they know the meaning of the word *credible*.

2. Help students understand that the word *credible* means believable. A credible witness is one who can be trusted to tell the truth.

3. Explain that the root word *cred* means believe. Then write the words *credit, incredible,* and *creed* on the chalkboard. Discuss the ways in which believability is associated with these words.

    Credit—If a merchant gives a customer credit, he believes that the customer will pay at a later date.

    Incredible—If a story or event is incredible, it cannot be believed.

    Creed—A creed is a statement of one's beliefs.

4. Ask the students to list other words containing the root *cred*. The students may offer words such as *discredit, credentials,* or *accreditation*.

5. Write the root *port* and the sentence, *The detectives found a portable television in the old house* on the board or chart. Ask students for the definition of the word *portable*. Explain to the class that the root *port* means carry.

6. Ask the students to list additional words containing the root *port*. The students may suggest words such as *transport, import, export,* or *deport*. Discuss the definition of each word and how the concepts of carrying or moving are associated with that word.

7. Distribute the "Unlocking Words" worksheet (pages 37–38). Ask students to read the paragraph at the top of the worksheet and complete the activity.

Skills and Strategies   *Student Worksheet*

Unlocking Words

One day Ryan and his younger sister, Nicole, were exploring the attic in their grandparents' house. "Hey Nicole," said Ryan, "I solved the mystery of why Grandpop won't go swimming with us. Here's an old newspaper with a picture and a story about Grandpop when he was a teenager. Listen to this."

> *Spectators at the Farmers' Fair were horrified when a car in which George Harris was riding hydroplaned on a wet road and slid into a pool. George escaped but he admitted that he was scared. "I'm hydrophobic," said George, "so I was very frightened when my car went into the water."*

"Huh?" said Nicole, "What does that mean?"

"I didn't know some of the words either," said Ryan, "but then I remembered that we learned how to take words apart in school last week. We can break the words apart and figure out what they mean. *Spec* means to watch so spectators are people who watch something. *Hydro* means water. When Grandpop's car hydroplaned, it slid on a wet road. *Phobia* means fear. Grandpop said he was hydrophobic so that means he is afraid of the water. That's why Grandpop doesn't like to swim with us or sail in our boat."

Using Clues to Predict a Word's Meaning

Like the students above, you can use root words to help you figure out the meaning of new words.

Root Word	Meaning
Hydro	Water
Spec	Watch, Look
Phobia	Fear
Mal	Bad
Bene	Good

Use this chart of root words to predict the meaning of each word in the chart on the next page. After you have written your predictions, find the meaning of each word in the dictionary.

Skills and Strategies   *Student Worksheet*

Unlocking Words (cont.)

New Word	Your Prediction	Dictionary Definition	Was your prediction correct?
1. hydrant			
2. hydrate			
3. dehydrate			
4. hydrology			
5. inspect			
6. spectacle			
7. spectrum			
8. spectacular			
9. phobic			
10. zoophobia			
11. arachnophobia			
12. claustrophobic			
13. malnutrition			
14. malpractice			
15. maltreated			
16. malformed			
17. benefit			
18. beneficial			
19. benefactor			
20. benign			

Skills and Strategies

Strange Sounding Words

Strange sounds in the night, creaking doors and running footsteps, whispers and echoes of unseen voices—there are many words to describe the sounds around us and these descriptive words can add to the drama and excitement of a mystery. Challenge your students to use their knowledge of root words to find descriptive words related to sounds.

Objective: Given a root word, students will compile a list of words which contain that root word.

Standard: Uses the general skills and strategies of the reading process

Benchmark: Uses word origins and derivations to understand word meaning

Skill Development: Using root words to determine the meaning of unfamiliar words

Organization: Whole class activity and small groups

Materials

- chalkboard and chalk, dry erase board and markers, or chart paper and markers
- kitchen timer

Procedure:

1. Write the words *telephone, microphone,* and *phonics* on a chalkboard, dry erase board, or chart paper. Ask students what these words have in common. (All of the words contain the root *phon.*) Discuss the meaning of each word and how it relates to the concept of sound.

Word	Definition
Telephone	The root *tele* means distance and the root *phon* means sound—A telephone enables a listener to hear sounds across a distance.
Microphone	The root *micro* means small and the root *phon* means sound—A microphone makes faint sounds louder.
Phonics	*Phonics* is the study of sounds that make up our language.

2. Ask students to suggest additional words containing the root *phon.* They might list words such as *megaphone, homophone, phoneme, saxophone, symphony,* or *phonograph.* Discuss the meaning of each word.

Skills and Strategies

Strange Sounding Words *(cont.)*

Procedure *(cont.)*

3. Introduce additional root words related to the concept of sound by copying the chart below onto the board or chart. Discuss the root words and their meanings with the class.

Root Word	Meaning
Aud	Hear
Voc	Call, Voice
Mem	Remember

Examples

Audiotape, Audible

Vocalist, Revocable

Memory, Memo

4. Divide the students into teams of four to five members and challenge each team to play "Root Word Challenge."

5. Begin with the first root word, *aud*. Set a kitchen timer for five to ten minutes, and ask each team to write as many words as possible using that root word. (Choose an appropriate time limit based on the needs and abilities of your particular class.)

6. When the timer rings, ask each group to write their words on the board or chart. Give the teams one point for each word they list. The team with the most points is the winner.

7. Repeat the procedure with the additional root words, *voc* and *mem*.

   Note: Some teachers may wish to have their students use a dictionary for this activity while other teachers may prefer to have their students rely on their own vocabulary and experiences. Make the adaptations which suit your specific group of students.

Making Predictions

Perplexing Predictions

Confident students make predictions as they read. They absorb information presented in a text, relate it to their own experiences, and predict logical conclusions. Predicting events in a narrative text, however, can be perplexing. Stories which follow a tired formula are predictable but those plots usually don't motivate the reader to turn the page. It is the book with cleverly surprising twists and turns that compel the reader to stay up late hiding under the bedcovers to learn the solution to a mystery.

Although teaching students to make predictions is a worthwhile use of instructional time, teachers must also help students understand that they have not failed when they are unable to accurately predict the end of a narrative. The best writers thwart their fans' attempts to predict the endings to their tales. While readers search for clues and weigh evidence, talented writers introduce new elements which move characters down unexpected paths. During reading instruction, students should be encouraged to make predictions and to support their predictions with events from the text. They should be prepared, however, to surrender their predictions to the talent of the writer.

Objective: Given a mystery text, students will search for clues and predict the ending of the mystery.

Standard: Uses the general skills and strategies of the reading process

Benchmark: Establishes and adjusts purposes for reading (e.g., to understand, interpret, enjoy, solve problems, predict outcomes, answer a specific question, form an opinion, skim for facts; to discover models for own writing)

Skill Development: Making and adjusting predictions

Organization: Whole-class and independent work

Materials

- short mystery story (Suggested title: *Five-Minute Mini-Mysteries* by Stan Smith)
- student copies of the "Perplexing Predictions" worksheet (page 43)
- mystery novels

Procedure

1. Read a short mystery to your class. Selections from *Five-Minute Mini Mysteries* by Stan Smith would be appropriate. These mysteries are only two to four pages in length and can be read aloud in five minutes or less.

    As you are reading, stop periodically to "think aloud." Make comments such as, "There's a good clue," or, "I think Borden is guilty because he lied about his trip." State your predictions as you are reading the mystery to the class.

Making Predictions

Perplexing Predictions (cont.)

Procedure (cont.)

2. Before revealing the solution to the mystery, stop and review the predictions you have made with the class. Discuss the clues that led you to make those predictions. Find evidence in the text to support your predictions. Then read the solution to the mystery. By reading the mystery orally and discussing your predictions, you have modeled a prediction strategy for your students.

   You and your students may have been successful in predicting the solution to the mystery. If you accurately predicted the solution, then you have taught your students to search for clues and examine evidence in a logical manner. If your predictions were inaccurate, you may have taught your students a different, equally valuable lesson.

   Often a reader is unable to predict the end of a mystery because a skilled writer has created unexpected twists and turns. If the predictions that you and your students made did not accurately reflect the solution to the mystery, ask the students to examine the reasons why you could not predict the solution. Did you miss clues or did the writer surprise you?

3. Ask students to discuss their favorite mysteries. Which did they enjoy more, the mysteries that they were able to solve or the mysteries in which the writer provided a surprise ending?

4. Tell the students that they will soon begin reading a new mystery. Encourage them to make predictions as they read. The students can use the "Perplexing Predictions" worksheet (page 43) to record their predictions as they read.

5. When the students have finished reading a mystery, use their completed "Perplexing Predictions" worksheets to discuss the predictions they made and the ways in which their predictions changed as they read more of the text.

Suggested Mystery Novels

- *Chasing Vermeer* by Blue Balliett
- *I'm Not Who You Think I Am* by Peg Kehret
- *Selections from the A to Z Mystery Series* by Ron Roy

Suggested Mystery Short Stories

- *Five Minute Mini-Mysteries* by Stan Smith
- *The Adventures of Sherlock Holmes* by Arthur Conan Doyle (adapted by Malvina G. Vogel)
- *Tales of O. Henry: Retold Timeless Classics* by Peg Hall

Making Predictions   *Student Worksheet*

Perplexing Predictions

Readers often try to predict the solutions to mystery novels by their favorite authors. Some writers leave clues to help their readers make predictions while other writers surprise their readers with unexpected twists and turns.

Select a mystery novel to read. As you are reading, you should record your predictions on this sheet.

Beginning Predictions

(*Complete this section after reading one to two chapters of the mystery novel.*)

Who do you think is the culprit? _____

What clues have led you to this prediction? _____

_____

_____

If you were the detective on this case, what questions would you ask? _____

_____

_____

Mid-Point Predictions

(*Complete this section when you reach the middle of the novel.*)

Do you still agree with your first prediction? _____

Do you want to change or adjust your predictions? What changes would you make? ___

_____

_____

What made you change your predictions? _____

_____

_____

Conclusions

(*Complete this section when you have finished reading the novel.*)

Did you predict the end of the mystery? _____

How did the writer surprise you? _____

_____

_____

Making Predictions

Clozing the Case

Detectives fill in the blanks to solve their cases. Reading and writing teachers can also use fill in the blank activities, known as cloze, to gather evidence about their students and to encourage descriptive writing.

Cloze is an informal assessment technique which can help you measure your students' abilities to use syntactical and semantic clues to fill in missing words in a passage. For example, you might select the following passage from a mystery novel:

Jenny ran into the street, searching for her missing dog. She hoped she could find him before it was too late.

You would then delete every fifth word to create a cloze passage which would test the students' comprehension.

Jenny ran into the _____ , searching for her missing _____ . She hoped she could _____ him before it was _____ late.

Students would be asked to read the passage and replace the blanks with appropriate words.

Cloze is usually used to test comprehension. This lesson presents a variation on the cloze technique which can be used to stimulate descriptive writing.

> **Objective:** Students will add descriptive words to sentences.
>
> **Standard:** Uses grammatical and mechanical conventions in written compositions
>
> **Benchmarks:** Uses nouns in written composition
> Uses verbs in written composition
> Uses adjectives in written composition
> Uses adverbs in written composition
>
> **Skill Development:** Descriptive writing, prediction
>
> **Organization:** Whole class and small groups

Materials
- chalkboard and chalk, dry erase board and markers, or chart paper and markers

Procedure

1. Write the following sentence on a chalkboard or dry erase board: *On a _____ night, three _____ men ran down the _____ .* Ask the students to suggest words to fill in the blanks. As the students offer words, write their suggestions under the appropriate blanks. Tell the students that there are many words which could appropriately fill the blanks in the sentence.

2. Divide the students into groups of three to five. Designate a space at the board for each group. On a separate section of the board, write the following sentence: *Ryan clutched the _____ and ran to tell his teacher what he found.* Tell the groups that they will have two minutes to list as many words as possible to complete that sentence. The group which has compiled the largest number of appropriate words is the winner.

Making Predictions

Clozing the Case (cont.)

Procedure *(cont.)*

3. Give the teams additional sentences such as:

   Eileen _____ through the icy streets to her car.

   Therese gathered the toys and ran _____ to her daughter.

   Ray found the old _____ and took it home.

   Andy threw the _____ through the old hoop.

4. Continue the activity by giving the teams sentences with multiple blanks such as:

   Harry fell down the _____ staircase and landed on a _____ .

   When Louise opened the _____ envelope, she found a _____ inside.

   The walls shook and the windows _____ as the storm _____ the house.

   The _____ dog barked when the _____ woman entered the house and grabbed the _____ .

Mysteries and Poetry

Mystery for Two Voices

A unique form of poetry, *Poems for Two Voices* enable students to respond to literature by identifying with the characters. Two students work together and each takes the role of one of the main characters. Each student writes stanzas from their character's viewpoint. The stanzas from both students are then written in two, side-by-side columns. The students give an oral presentation in which each student reads the stanzas representing their characters.

Poems for Two Voices enable students to consider the viewpoints and motivations of each character. Students have an opportunity to express themselves orally and in writing. In this lesson, students will create *Poems for Two Voices* representing the two main characters in a mystery novel they have read.

Objective: Students will work with a partner to write a *Poem for Two Voices.*

Standard: Uses reading skills and strategies to understand and interpret a variety of literary texts

Benchmarks: Makes connections between the motives of characters or the causes for complex events in texts and/or his or her own life

Understands the use of language in literary works to convey mood, images, and meaning

Skill Development: Forming inferences, writing skills, cooperative learning

Organization: Whole-class activity and pairs

Materials

- paper and pencils
- overhead transparency of "Poem for Two Voices–*Cinderella and the Mystery of the Glass Slipper*" (page 47)

Procedure

1. Read the *Cinderella and the Mystery of the Glass Slipper* example (page 47) to your students. Using an overhead transparency of the poem, have one student read the role of Cinderella and another student read the lines of Prince Charming. Provide time for these students to perform the poem for their classmates. Tell the students that they will work in pairs to create a poem featuring two main characters from a mystery they have read.

2. Have students form pairs. Ask each pair to identify the two main characters in a mystery they have read. Who caused a problem in the story? Who solved the problem? Each partner should take the role of one of the main characters in the mystery.

3. The students should fold a sheet of paper to create two columns. Each student should write the lines for his or her character in one of the columns. Students should practice reading their lines orally.

4. Provide time for each pair to perform their poem for the class.

Poem for Two Voices

Cinderella and the Mystery of the Glass Slipper

Cinderella	Prince Charming
I must run. The clock is striking midnight.	
	She's gone. Where did she go?
Where is my shoe?	
	What will I do?
I must find my shoe.	
	I just have her shoe.
Only that shoe will fit. It leads to my prince. I must find my shoe.	Only that girl will do. She will be my bride. I just have her shoe.
I must find my shoe.	I just have her shoe.

Mysteries and Poetry

Puzzling Poems

After reading mysteries and investigating unusual situations, your students may be ready to write their own puzzling poems!

Objective: After reading mysteries, students will write Who Am I? poems based on the mysteries.

Standard: Uses the general skills and strategies of the writing process

Benchmark: Writes in response to literature

Skill Development: Use of descriptive vocabulary

Organization: Whole-class and independent work

Materials
- selection of mystery novels

Procedure

1. Display copies of mysteries that the class has read. Review the mysteries by asking the students to guess the answers to Who Am I? poems.

> **Example:**
> *Someone is following me.*
> *She hides nearby, she hides behind trees.*
> *She follows my bus, she calls on the phone.*
> *I'm afraid, I'm alone.*
> *I am _____ .*

Solution: Ginger in *I'm Not Who You Think I Am* by Peg Kehret

2. Ask each student to select a favorite character or event from a mystery that he or she has read recently. The students should then create Who Am I? poems based on the characters or events they selected.

3. Provide time for the students to read and share their poems with classmates. You may wish to have the students type their poems and make a class book of the Who Am I? poems.

Literature-Based Mysteries

What's Up, Sherlock? Learning about Sherlock Holmes

The great detective, Sherlock Holmes, is part of our literary heritage and many of the expressions we use today come from the 66 short stories and four novels written by his creator, Arthur Conan Doyle. A study of Sherlock Holmes' stories will help your students understand the roots of the mystery genre and encourage them to use their powers of observation.

Objective: After reading a Sherlock Holmes short story, students will identify the story's protagonist and antagonist.

Standard: Uses reading skills and strategies to understand and interpret a variety of literary texts

Benchmark: Understands elements of character development

Skill Development: Identifying character elements, using literary terminology

Organization: Whole class activity and independent work

Materials

- overhead transparency of "Background on Sherlock Holmes" (page 50), optional
- student copies of the "Sherlock Holmes" student worksheet (page 51)

Procedure

1. Begin by asking the students if they are familiar with the expressions, "What's up Sherlock?" or "Elementary, my dear Watson." Ask if anyone knows where these expressions originated. Students who know that these expressions can be traced to the Sherlock Holmes' stories could be invited to give the class background information on Sherlock Holmes.

2. Use the background information on page 50 to tell the class about Sherlock Holmes. You may want to display the page on an overhead projector so students can read along. Tell the class that you will be reading several Sherlock Holmes' stories.

3. Select a Sherlock Holmes story to read to the class. (*The Red-Headed League* would be an appropriate choice for students in grades 4–8.) Teachers should be able to find copies of Sherlock Holmes' stories in the school or community library. Full text of the stories is also available on the Internet at **http://www.yoak.com/sherlock/stories/index.html**

4. After reading a Sherlock Holmes short story, write the terms *protagonist* and *antagonist* on the chalkboard. Discuss the meaning of these terms and help the students identify the protagonist and antagonist in the story you read to them.

5. Ask each student to read one additional Sherlock Holmes story and complete the "Sherlock Holmes Worksheet" (page 51).

Background on Sherlock Holmes

Sherlock Holmes

Literature's master detective, Sherlock Holmes, solved crimes by considering evidence, the physical and social characteristics of suspects, and his own background experiences. Sherlock Holmes lived at 221B Baker Street in London and worked in harmony with the criminal justice officials of Scotland Yard. Holmes had an able assistant, Dr. John Watson, with whom he often worked and discussed his cases.

Sherlock Holmes was the invention of writer Arthur Conan Doyle. A native of Scotland, Doyle was trained as a physician, but he enjoyed writing novels and short stories in his spare time. Doyle based his protagonist, Sherlock Holmes, on the professors he met during his medical training. Doyle admired his professors' keen sense of observation and he transferred these qualities to his literary character, Sherlock Holmes. Readers gave the Sherlock Holmes' stories such credibility that police officers often asked writer Arthur Conan Doyle to assist them as they tried to solve crimes.

Literature-Based Mysteries *Student Worksheet*

Sherlock Holmes Worksheet

Arthur Conan Doyle wrote 66 short stories and four novels about the clever detective Sherlock Holmes and his curious assistant, Dr. John Watson. These tales begin with strangers asking Sherlock Holmes to help them solve their problems or dilemmas. The character bringing his or her problem to Sherlock Holmes is called the protagonist. The character causing the problem or creating a bad situation is called the antagonist.

Read a Sherlock Holmes mystery. Think about the characters you meet in that mystery and answer these questions:

Sherlock Holmes Mystery Title: _____

_____

Who is the protagonist in this mystery? _____

_____

What is his or her occupation? _____

Where does the protagonist live? _____

Write two to three sentences to describe the protagonist. _____

_____

_____

Who is the antagonist in this mystery? _____

_____

What is her or her occupation? _____

Where does the antagonist live? _____

Write two to three sentences to describe the antagonist. _____

_____

_____

_____

What is the protagonist's problem or dilemma? _____

_____

_____

What clues help Sherlock Holmes solve the mystery? _____

_____

_____

Literature-Based Mysteries

The Power of Observation

One of Sherlock Holmes' most impressive traits was his ability to infer a person's occupation and habits with one quick glance. Help your students develop their own powers of observation by examining pictures in newspapers and magazines.

Objective: Students will use a newspaper or magazine picture to write a character description.

Standard: Uses the general skills and strategies of the writing process

Benchmark: Writes descriptive compositions

Skill Development: Visual literacy, observation, writing skills

Organization: Whole class activity and independent work

Materials

- selection of Sherlock Holmes short stories
- newspaper and/or magazine pictures of people

Procedure

1. After reading a Sherlock Holmes short story to the class, initiate a discussion of Sherlock Holmes' powers of observation. Sherlock Holmes always observed the clothing and habits of clients and suspects to solve his cases. Ask the class if they believe that someone's clothing, hairstyle, or facial expression can be used as a clue to solve a case.

2. Distribute newspaper and magazine pictures of various unknown people to the students. Ask each student to observe the clothes, jewelry, and hairstyle of the people in the pictures. What can these things tell the students about the people in the pictures? Perhaps a favorite basketball or football jersey will reveal clues about a person's hometown or interests. The clothing may indicate a person's occupation or hobby.

3. Ask students to write a paragraph indicating the assumptions they have made about the people in the pictures. For example, a student might write: *"This person is very athletic. She is wearing a tee-shirt with the name of a softball tournament that was held last week. Her sneakers look dusty so I think she has been playing softball in a dry field."*

4. Invite the students to pretend that they are Arthur Conan Doyle and that they are creating a character for a mystery novel. The students should write a character description based upon their observations of the people in the pictures.

Literature-Based Mysteries

The Eleventh Hour: Time to Start a Mystery

Clocks stop, stairs creak, and curious figures scurry in the darkness. Mysteries grow at the 11th hour, a time when tricksters put the finishing touches on their pranks.

Read aloud *The Eleventh Hour: A Curious Mystery* by Graeme Base to spark your students' interest in mysteries. The shared enjoyment of this picture book read aloud can unite the class and encourage students to read, respond, and share additional intriguing mysteries.

Objective: Students will follow written instructions to solve a mystery.

Standard: Uses reading skills and strategies to understand and interpret a variety of literary texts.

Benchmark: Understands complex elements of plot development (e.g., cause-and-effect relationships; use of subplots, parallel episodes, and climax; development of conflict and resolution)

Skill Development: Forms inferences, follows written directions

Organization: Whole class activity and small groups

Materials
- one copy of *The Eleventh Hour: A Curious Mystery* by Graeme Base for each group of four to six students

Procedure
1. Show the cover of *The Eleventh Hour: A Curious Mystery* and tell the class that this mystery is written as a narrative poem, a poem that tells a story. Tell students that this is the story of an elaborate birthday party. One guest at the party plays a nasty trick on the host and the other guests. Challenge the students to listen and watch for clues to identify the trickster and the scheme.
2. Read *The Eleventh Hour: A Curious Mystery*, to the class. After the story has been read, allow the students to give their general reactions to the story, but don't discuss specific clues.
3. Tell the class that they will work together in groups to solve the mystery. Divide the students into groups of four to six. Give each group a copy of the book.
4. In their groups, the students should discuss the story and name the chief suspects. Who do the students think stole the feast? Why? What evidence points to that suspect?
5. Graeme Base, the author of *The Eleventh Hour: A Curious Mystery,* provides instructions for solving the mystery. At the end of the book there is a sealed section titled, *The Eleventh Hour: A Curious Mystery, The Inside Story*. The information contained in the sealed section can serve as a self-directed lesson in finding clues. Working together, each group should use these instructions to solve the mystery.
6. After each group has solved the mystery, provide time for the class to discuss the story. Did any of the students guess who the thief was? Did the author leave appropriate clues? Discuss the steps the students took to solve the mystery. Have they gained skills that will help them solve future mysteries?

Literature-Based Mysteries

The Mysteries of Harris Burdick

Chris Van Allsburg's imaginative work *The Mysteries of Harris Burdick* provides an intriguing premise and 14 startling drawings to inspire students to create their own stories.

In the book's introduction, readers learn that a writer, Harris Burdick, brought 14 unusual drawings to a book publisher in the hopes of having his work published. Mr. Burdick told the publisher that these pictures illustrated 14 short stories that he had written. When the publisher expressed interest, Burdick gave him the drawings and agreed to return the next day with the stories. Unfortunately, Harris Burdick never returned. The publisher was left with the pictures and a longing to read the accompanying stories.

The mysterious events surrounding these pictures can raise questions for your students and motivate them to write their own mysterious adventure stories.

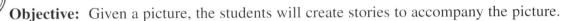

Objective: Given a picture, the students will create stories to accompany the picture.

Standard: Uses viewing skills and strategies to understand and interpret visual media

Benchmarks: Understands how language choice is used to enhance visual media
Understands reasons for varied interpretations of visual media

Standard: Uses the general skills and strategies of the writing process

Benchmarks: Writes narrative accounts, such as short stories
Writes in response to literature

Skill Development: Visual literacy skills, creative writing

Organization: Whole class and small groups

Materials

- copy of *The Mysteries of Harris Burdick* by Chris Van Allsburg

    (*Note:* There are several editions of *The Mysteries of Harris Burdick*. This text is available in an 8½" by 11" hardback or paperback picture book format which would be suitable for a classroom library or for working with individuals or small groups. Teachers, however, may prefer the portfolio edition which has loose oversized sheets that can be displayed for whole class discussions and writing projects. The portfolio edition also includes an extra drawing and an updated introduction by the author.)

Procedure

1. Tell the class that you are going to present them with a mystery. Read the introduction to *The Mysteries of Harris Burdick*.

2. Discuss the intriguing puzzle presented in the introduction. Why didn't Harris Burdick ever return to the book publisher's office? What happened to the stories that Harris Burdick wrote? Did Harris Burdick write additional stories?

Literature-Based Mysteries

The Mysteries of Harris Burdick *(cont.)*

Procedure *(cont.)*

3. The first picture shows a sleeping boy and the words, *Is he the one?* Discuss this picture with the class and invite them to suggest stories to accompany the picture.

4. Divide the students into groups of four and assign one picture to each group. Encourage the students to write stories to accompany their assigned picture.

5. Provide time for each group to share their story with the entire class.

Sharing the Stories

There are many ways for your students to share their stories. Here are some suggestions:

- **Internet Publishing**

    The Mysteries of Harris Burdick has inspired teachers and students around the world to create their own answers to these puzzling drawings. There are now many websites which publish students' responses to these pictures. Teachers can enter the title, *The Mysteries of Harris Burdick,* into a search engine to find classroom webpages and writing projects which encourage students to submit and publish their original stories based on this book.

- **Bulletin Board Displays**

    Use pictures from the Portfolio Edition of *The Mysteries of Harris Burdick* to create a bulletin board display in the classroom or school hallway. Invite students to post their original stories under the corresponding pictures.

- **Class Book**

    Compile your students' stories into a class book. This book could be made available in the school library for other classes to read and enjoy as they explore *The Mysteries of Harris Burdick.* The book could be made by placing all of your students' stories into a three-ring binder, or you may have access to a binding machine in your school or local copying center.

Literature-Based Mysteries

Drawing a Mystery

Using *The Mysteries of Harris Burdick* by Chris Van Allsburg as a model, invite your students to create their own pictures to draw intrigue and suspicion.

Objectives: Students will draw pictures to inspire mysteries.

Given a picture, students will write a mystery based on the picture.

Standard: Uses viewing skills and strategies to understand and interpret visual media

Benchmark: Understands how language choice is used to enhance visual media

Standard: Uses the general skills and strategies of the writing process

Benchmark: Writes narrative accounts, such as poems and stories

Skill Development: Drawing, writing narrative accounts

Organization: Pairs and individual work

Materials

- a copy of *The Mysteries of Harris Burdick* by Chris Van Allsburg

Procedure

1. Read or review *The Mysteries of Harris Burdick* with your class. Discuss the ways in which the author and illustrator, Chris Van Allsburg, used his drawings and captions to arouse the curiosity of his readers.

2. Tell the students that they will have an opportunity to draw and share their own original pictures with their classmates. Ask the students to think about an unusual building, person, or event that raised questions for them. Encourage each student to draw a picture representing that mysterious object or occurrence. Help the students to write intriguing, single-sentence captions for their pictures.

3. Ask students to exchange their pictures with a classmate. The students should then write a mystery based on the pictures they have received. As an alternative, teachers might wish to exchange drawings with other classes in their school or with classes from another school.

4. Provide time for the students to share their stories with the students who drew the pictures.

Alternative Activity: Rather than asking students to draw pictures, teachers may wish to use old photographs or magazine and newspaper pictures as story starters.

Literature-Based Mysteries

The Mystery Picture Party

After reading and discussing *The Mysteries of Harris Burdick,* your students may crave more mysterious adventures. Draw your students into a mystery by staging a Mystery Picture Party in your classroom.

Objective: Given a picture, students will write an original mystery based on the picture.

Standard: Uses the general skills and strategies of the writing process

Benchmark: Writes narrative accounts, such as short stories

Organization: Whole class activity and small groups

Preparation

- The Mystery Picture Party requires students to play the roles of the narrator, school principal, and school secretary. Identify individuals who can perform a scene together and discreetly ask them to become the cast of the Mystery Picture Party.

Materials

- old photographs or magazine pictures (1940s–1950s)
- wooden box to use as a time capsule
- costumes for students to play the roles of the narrator, school principal, and school secretary
- "Script for the Mystery Picture Party" (page 58)
- copies of the "Mystery Picture Party" worksheet (page 59)

Procedure

1. Seat the class in groups of four to six to await the beginning of the Mystery Picture Party.

2. Assemble the cast of the Mystery Picture Party. A narrator, Mrs. Brady, the school principal, and Mrs. Harris, the school secretary, will be needed for the cast.

3. The cast should enter the front of the room, dressed in costumes, and prepare to begin the Mystery Picture Party. The narrator opens the Mystery Picture Party by reading the script (page 58). The two remaining cast members, Mrs. Brady and Mrs. Harris, should act out the script as the narrator reads.

4. The students playing Mrs. Brady and Mrs. Harris should give one photograph and one "Mystery Picture Party" worksheet (page 59) to each group of students seated at their desks or tables.

5. The narrator should ask each group to examine their assigned picture and complete the worksheet. Students can use their imagination to describe the people and situations shown in the photographs.

6. Invite each group to read their story to the class.

7. Create a mystery party atmosphere in the classroom by awarding prizes in categories such as the scariest story, most unusual story, or most historically accurate story.

Literature-Based Mysteries

Script for the Mystery Picture Party

While cleaning her office at the Greenwich School, Mrs. Brady, the school principal, found an old wooden box hidden on the bottom shelf of her closet. When she opened the box, Mrs. Brady found eight pictures and a note which read:

> *Dear Students of the Future,*
>
> *The 1952 graduating class of the Greenwich School has hidden this time capsule to share our memories with you. Inside the box you will find pictures that depict our happy times with family and friends as well as our frustrations and disappointments. We hope that you will use these pictures to remember us and think about the ways in which the world has changed since we attended Greenwich School.*
>
> *Good luck in your studies. Make the world a better place.*
>
> *Sincerely,*
>
> *The 1952 Graduating Class of Greenwich School*

There were no names, dates, or descriptions on the pictures. Mrs. Brady showed the pictures to her secretary, Mrs. Harris. Mrs. Harris had worked at the school for many years but she never knew that a time capsule had been hidden in the principal's office.

Mrs. Brady and Mrs. Harris have decided to bring these pictures to you, the current students, to help them unravel the mystery of these photographs. Perhaps you know the identities and stories of these former students.

Literature-Based Mysteries   *Student Worksheet*

The Mystery Picture Party

Group Members: _____
_____

Name the characters in the picture you have been given. _____
_____
_____

Give the ages of the characters. _____
_____
_____

Describe the setting of the picture. _____
_____
_____
_____

What events are taking place in the picture? _____
_____
_____
_____

What problems might occur in this situation? _____
_____
_____
_____

How could the characters solve their problems? _____
_____
_____
_____

Create a story based on the picture. Be prepared to share your story with the entire class.

Literature-Based Mysteries

Two Sides to Every Story

There are two sides to every story! When solving a mystery, an investigator must listen to all sides and keep a fair and open mind. Encourage your students to consider opposing viewpoints by discussing the feelings and motivations of well-known characters in traditional tales.

> **Objective:** Students will write a new ending to a traditional tale.
> **Standard:** Uses the general skills and strategies of the writing process
> **Benchmark:** Writes in response to literature
> **Skill Development:** Speaking and listening skills, creative writing
> **Organization:** Whole class and small group

Materials

- *The True Story of the 3 Little Pigs!* by John Scieszka

Procedure

1. Ask the students if they have ever heard the expression, "There are two sides to every story". Encourage the students to discuss the meaning of this expression and the times in their lives when they have felt that someone was not listening to their side of a story.

2. Read *The True Story of the 3 Little Pigs!* to your students. The traditional tale of the three little pigs tells the story from the pigs' viewpoint. John Scieszka's version gives the wolf's account of the events.

3. Use the examples on the chart below to remind your students of other traditional tales in which one or more of the characters have been portrayed as villains.

Traditional Tale	Villainous Character
Cinderella	Wicked Stepmother and Stepsisters
Hansel and Gretel	The Witch
Jack and the Beanstalk	The Giant
Wizard of Oz	Wicked Witch of the West

4. Divide your students into four groups. Using the chart above, assign one traditional tale to each group. Ask each group to think about the actions of the villainous characters in their assigned traditional tales. Were these characters really villains or were they merely misunderstood like the wolf in *The True Story of the 3 Little Pigs!?*

5. Using *The True Story of the 3 Little Pigs!* as a model, each group should write a new version of their assigned traditional tale. The new version should tell the story from the alleged villain's point of view. (Example: Cinderella's stepsisters would insist that Cinderella was too young to tag along with them everywhere and she should not have sneaked off to the ball when she wasn't invited. They would say that Cinderella was rude to her stepmother and didn't follow her rules.)

6. Provide time for each group to share their new version with the class.

Literature-Based Mysteries

Mystery Reviews

Confident readers make personal connections with the texts they are reading and they welcome opportunities to share their thoughts and opinions. Invite your students to write reviews of the mystery books and short stories they have read. Writing reviews will enable the students to reflect upon their reading and to publish their comments.

Objective: Students will write a review of a mystery they have read.

Standard: Uses the general skills and strategies of the writing process

Benchmark: Writes in response to literature

Skill Development: Writing a summary

Organization: Whole class activity and independent work

Materials

- student copies of the "Review a Mystery" worksheet (page 62)

- reviews of novels which the students have already read: Reviews can often be found on the back cover of a novel. These reviews are usually written at an appropriate level for fourth to eighth grade students to read independently. Newspapers often offer reviews of juvenile novels as well as adult titles. Periodicals for teachers, such as *Teaching PreK-8* and *Instructor*, usually include reviews of new books for children and young adults. An excellent source of reviews is the *Children's Choices Project*, published each year in the October issue of *The Reading Teacher*. Every year 10,000 students across the United States participate in a process in which they read and discuss newly published trade books, vote to select their favorites, and write reviews. Books are grouped into the categories of Beginning and Young Readers (Grades K–2), Intermediate Readers (Grades 3–4), and Advanced Readers (Grades 5–6). Teachers can find more information and the most recent listing of the *Children's Choices Project* selections by visiting the website for the *International Reading Association* at **http://www.reading.org** and entering the term *Children's Choices Project* in the search box.

Procedure

1. After the class has read a mystery, read a review of that mystery with your students. Ask your students if they agree with the reviewer's comments on the mystery novel. Did the reviewer overlook any important aspects of the book? Did your students and the reviewer interpret the characters' actions in the same way? Would your students give the mystery the same rating that the reviewer gave?

2. Invite your students to use the "Review a Mystery" worksheet (page 62) to write their own reviews of mysteries they have read.

   Post copies of your students' reviews in your school or classroom library. Their reviews will help other students select reading material.

Literature-Based Mysteries *Student Worksheet*

Review a Mystery

What have you been reading? Did you read a suspense novel that you would like to recommend to your friends? Did you read a mystery that was so predictable that it was not worth your time? After reading a novel or short story, readers often state their opinions of the text in a brief written or oral statement called a review. A review gives a summary of the text and the reasons why someone else should or should not read it.

Use this worksheet to begin writing a review for a mystery that you have read recently.

Mystery Title: _____

Author: _____ Date of Publication: _____

Give a brief summary of the mystery. Describe the setting and main characters. (Note: Remember that the people who will be reading your review have not yet read the book or short story you are summarizing. They are deciding whether it would interest them. Your summary must not reveal the ending of the mystery!)

Summary: _____

_____

_____

_____

_____

_____

Do you recommend this mystery? _____

Why or why not? _____

_____

_____

Recommendation: _____

_____

_____

Rate this mystery on a scale from 1 to 5 where 1 is the lowest possible score and 5 is the highest possible score. For example, if you thought that this was a terrible story with a weak plot, give it a 1. If you believe that this was an intriguing mystery with fascinating characters, give it a 5. Give the story a score of 2, 3, or 4 if you feel it falls in the middle of the range.

Rating: ☐

Mysterious Oral Reading

Shivering Mystery Theater

Our grandparents huddled close to the radio and listened in rapture to mysterious tales of *The Shadow* and *The Green Hornet*. In later years we gathered at slumber parties and campsites to scare our friends with ghost stories and tales we swore were really true. Oral storytelling has been a powerful force to unite generations. Help your students join the league of storytellers by inviting them to tell a mystery story.

Objective: The students will read a mystery selection orally for their peers.

Standard: Uses listening and speaking strategies for different purposes

Benchmark: Makes oral presentations to the class

Standard: Uses the general skills and strategies of the reading process

Benchmark: Establishes and adjusts purposes for reading

Skill Development: Fluency, listening

Organization: Whole-class activity, independent work, and pairs

Materials

- a selection of mystery texts
- student copies of the "Shivering Mystery Theater Rubric" (page 65)

Procedure

1. Gather the class for a read-aloud. Read a brief selection such as the tantalizing first few pages of a mystery novel or an excerpt from *Five Minute Mini-Mysteries* by Stan Smith. As you read aloud, you are giving your students a model of fluent oral reading. Be sure to practice before reading aloud so that you can emphasize exciting portions and project your voice.

2. Place a selection of mystery audiobooks and accompanying text versions in a classroom independent reading center. (You may be able to borrow the audiobooks from a community or school library.) Students can listen and read along independently, in small groups, or in pairs.

3. After students have listened to several mystery selections read aloud, distribute copies of the "Shivering Mystery Theater Rubric" (page 65) and invite students to perform their own mystery readings. Tell students that they should read the criteria on the rubric and consider those elements as they practice their oral reading. Each student should select a brief passage (one to two pages of text). It is not necessary for the students to read an entire mystery orally. The purpose of the lesson is to give your students oral reading practice and to entice their listeners to read these mysteries independently.

Mysterious Oral Reading

Shivering Mystery Theater (cont.)

Procedure *(cont.)*

4. Provide time for the students to practice independently and with a partner. When working with a partner, the students should use the "Shivering Mystery Theater Rubric" to give their partners feedback on the oral reading.

5. Invite students to perform their oral readings for the entire class. The students may wish to record their readings on an audiotape. The tapes could be placed in the classroom independent reading center for students to enjoy during a free period.

Mysterious Oral Reading   *Student Worksheet*

Shivering Mystery Theater Rubric

	Yes/No	Comments
Did the reader speak clearly?		
Did the reader speak at an appropriate pace (not too fast, not too slow)?		
Did the reader use an appropriate volume (not too loud, not too soft)?		
Did the reader select an interesting passage?		
Did the reader use appropriate expression?		
Did the reader have good posture when he or she stood before the audience?		

Mysterious Oral Reading

Back Cover Voices

Publishers often place intriguing summaries on the back covers of popular trade books. These concise, captivating summaries can motivate reluctant students to read. The summaries can also serve as a quick source of oral reading material to be used in rereading activities.

Objective: The students will read story summaries aloud to their classmates.

Standard: Uses the general skills and strategies of the reading process

Benchmark: Establishes and adjusts purposes for reading

Skill Development: Fluency

Organization: Whole-class activity, small groups, and pairs

Materials

- selection of mystery trade books

Procedure

1. Select a mystery trade book. Show it to your class. Discuss the cover illustrations and invite the class to make predictions about the mystery. Read the summary on the back cover to the class. (Use expression! You are modeling fluent oral reading for your students.)

2. Tell the class that publishers often place intriguing summaries on the back covers of books to lure readers. This is a type of advertising that the publisher uses to attract readers.

3. Distribute copies of several different popular mystery trade books. (For example, in a class with 25 students, you may wish to distribute copies of five different books.) Encourage students to examine the covers and make predictions.

4. Tell the students to silently read the story summary on the back covers of the books they have been given. Then tell the students that it will be their job to read a summary with so much expression that their classmates will want to read that book.

5. Students will need to practice reading the summaries many times to give an expressive, exciting oral reading. This will give them an authentic purpose for rereading and will help the students become fluent readers.

6. Students may wish to work in small groups or with a partner to practice reading a story summary.

7. After the students have practiced, invite them to read the back cover summaries for their classmates.

8. The lively oral readings might inspire the students to read the complete novels. Make the books accessible for the students to read independently.

The Mystery Series

Did you read Nancy Drew books when you were growing as a reader? Did you sneak the books under the covers at night, pack them in your schoolbag and suitcase, and stash them in the car for long trips during school vacations? Did you go to the library looking for the next book in the series?

Perhaps the saddest moment for us as readers is when we come to the end of a good book. We are reluctant to leave the intriguing characters and places we have come to know to continue with our schoolwork and daily activities.

Fortunately, detectives appearing in mystery series, such as *Nancy Drew* and the *Hardy Boys*, invite readers to share their adventures through a series of novels. When we reach the last page of a great book, we know that there is another adventure waiting for us in the library.

Mystery series offer readers a chance to continue their relationship with their favorite literary characters. Series enable readers to develop a familiarity with characters, locations, and an author's style. Readers know what to expect and they can apply their background knowledge to each new book in a series.

You can hook the reluctant readers in your classroom by introducing them to mystery series such as the *A to Z Mysteries, Sammy Keyes, Nancy Drew, The Hardy Boys,* and *The Boxcar Children.* The activities in this section give suggestions for creating literature circles in which students have an opportunity to discuss their favorite mystery series. The students are also encouraged to write an original mystery starring their favorite detective from a mystery series. An annotated list of mystery series is provided, offering suggestions for intriguing mystery series. The series range in difficulty from a second grade reading level to seventh grade and beyond.

The Mystery Series

Favorite Mystery Series

Motivate reluctant readers and reward voracious readers by creating literature circles in which the students can read and discuss their favorite mystery series.

Objective: Students will read and discuss selections from a mystery series.

Standard: Uses the general skills and strategies of the reading process

Benchmark: Reflects on what has been learned after reading and formulates ideas, opinions, and personal responses

Skill Development: Fluency, forming inferences

Organization: Whole-class activity and small groups

Materials

- chalkboard and chalk, dry erase board and markers, or chart paper and markers
- selections from a mystery series
- copies of the "Favorite Mystery Series" worksheet (page 69)

Procedure

1. Bring selections of popular mystery series such as the *American Girl* mysteries, *A to Z Mysteries*, *Nancy Drew*, *The Hardy Boys*, *The Boxcar Children*, and *Trixie Belden*, to the classroom. Ask the class if they are familiar with these series.

2. Initiate a discussion of popular mystery series with the entire class. Ask the students to name mystery series that they enjoy. List the titles on the chalkboard, dry erase board, or chart paper.

3. Have students complete the "Favorite Mystery Series" worksheet (page 69).

4. Using the list on the chalkboard, designate an area of the classroom for each mystery series. Tell the students to sit in the area designated for their favorite mystery series. (Some students may not have read any of the series listed. Send a few of those students to each group. The groups can then tell those students about their favorite series and possibly inspire the undecided students to try a few of those books.)

5. Tell the class that you will provide time for them to meet in their groups to discuss their favorite mystery series.

The Mystery Series   *Student Worksheet*

Favorite Mystery Series

Sometimes we find a book that is so good we are sad when we come to the end! We wish that the book could go on and on. Fortunately, some writers have written many books about the same characters. There are several *Harry Potter* books in which we can share magical adventures with the young wizard. Great detectives such as *Nancy Drew* and *The Hardy Boys* appear in over 50 books so we can keep solving mysteries.

Use this worksheet to discuss your favorite mystery series with your friends. Think about your favorite mystery series and answer the questions below. Then meet with classmates who enjoy the same mystery series. Share your answers and discuss your favorite adventures.

1. Favorite Mystery Series:

   _____

2. Who are the main characters in that series?

   _____

   _____

3. Who is your favorite character in that series? Why?

   _____

   _____

   _____

4. Where do the stories take place?

   _____

   _____

5. What is your favorite episode in the series? Why?

   _____

   _____

   _____

   _____

The Mystery Series

A New Adventure Starring My Favorite Detective

Familiarity with characters and places can help young writers create original tales. Invite your students to create an original short story based on a character from a favorite mystery series.

Objective: The students will write a short story based on a character from a mystery series.

Standard: Uses the general skills and strategies of the writing process

Benchmark: Writes in response to literature

Skill Development: Use of descriptive vocabulary, improved sentence structure

Organization: Independent work

Materials

- selections from mystery series
- copies of the "A New Adventure Starring My Favorite Detective" worksheet (page 71)

Procedure

1. Display selections from several mystery series and initiate a discussion with your class. What are their favorite mystery series? Who are their favorite characters? What types of adventures do these characters have?

2. Discuss the ways in which some mystery series, such as *Nancy Drew* and *The Hardy Boys*, were written. These series were the creation of Edward Stratemeyer. Stratemeyer didn't write all of the stories alone. He devised plots, created outlines, and then hired writers to complete the stories. Although the covers list Carolyn Keene as the author of the Nancy Drew books and Franklin W. Dixon as the author of the Hardy Boys series, these were pseudonyms assigned to the books by Stratemeyer. Carolyn Keene and Franklin W. Dixon never existed.

3. Ask your students to pretend that they have been hired to write another adventure in their favorite mystery series. The students should select a character such as Trixie Belden, Nancy Drew, or Encyclopedia Brown, and use the "A New Adventure Staring My Favorite Detective" worksheet (page 71) to write a story based on that character. Distribute the worksheets and allow time for the students to write. Provide time during the writing period for the students to read drafts to their peers to receive feedback on their writing.

The Mystery Series Student Worksheet

A New Adventure Starring My Favorite Detective

When we read mystery series, we come to know the characters and often think of new adventures for them to pursue. Write an original adventure for your favorite character from a mystery series.

A good mystery writer outlines the story before he or she begins to write. Use this chart to make an outline for your mystery.

1. _____

2. _____

Mystery Series: _____

Main Character(s): _____

3. Setting for my original story (give place, year): _____

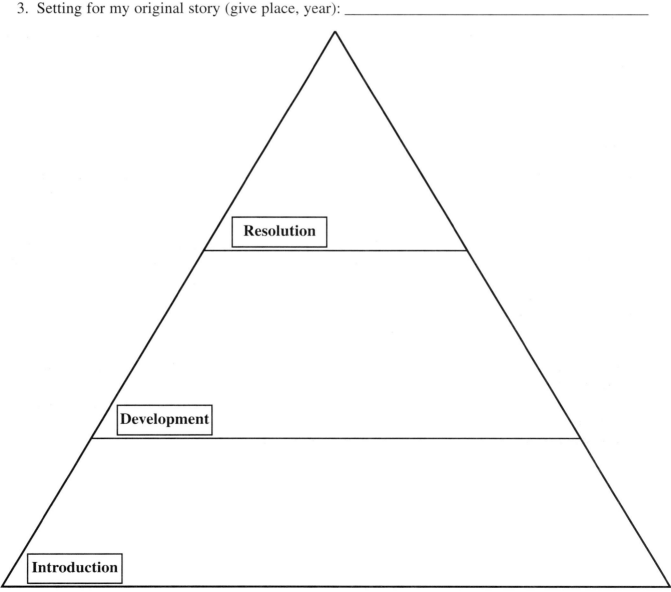

© Teacher Created Resources, Inc.   71   #3609 Writing and Reading Mysteries

The Mystery Series

Another Exciting Episode: Mystery Series to Explore

The list that follows presents mystery series that can be found in libraries, bookstores, and schools today. The list contains books on fourth to eighth grade reading levels as well as books on a second grade level for those older students who may struggle with word recognition and/or comprehension.

Popular Mystery Series to Explore

Alex Rider Adventures by Anthony Horowitz

In these fast paced mysteries, fourteen year old Alex Rider shows the skill and cunning of James Bond, as well as the bravery and adventurous spirit of Indiana Jones. Alex often misses school because he has been reluctantly recruited by organizations such as the CIA to fight crime throughout the world. In each novel in the series, Alex faces gripping adventures as he travels the globe to make the world safe for others. These books will encourage students to stay up late to learn how Alex defeats criminals.

Sammy Keyes Mysteries by Wendelin Van Draanen

Sammy Keyes is an outspoken, adventurous seventh grade girl who solves mysteries as she wanders the treacherous halls of middle school. This thirteen-year-old heroine lives secretly with her grandmother in a senior citizens only apartment complex. The books present a subtle message of respect for the elderly as they explore Sammy's relationship with her grandmother and her grandmother's peers. *The Sammy Keyes Mystery Series,* appropriate for 11 to 14 year old readers, offers perplexing mysteries and warm humor.

Five Minute Mysteries (Various authors)

This series for grades seven and up provides short mysteries for students to read and solve. Students may enjoy working in teams to read and solve the mysteries.

History Mysteries from American Girl (Various authors)

Suggested for students over age ten, these works of historical fiction offer readers an opportunity to visit memorable events in history. The books explore topics such as the ride of the Pony Express, the 1906 San Francisco Earthquake, the Civil War, and World War I. At the conclusion of each book, there is a section containing facts on the time period, location, and real-life characters who appeared in the book. These sections help teachers pair literary works with topics students may be studying in their social studies or science classes.

Mystic Lighthouse Mysteries by Laura E. Williams

Eleven year old twins Jen and Zeke live with their Aunt Bee in a lighthouse which has been converted to a bed and breakfast. The *Mystic Lighthouse Mysteries* follow the twins' adventures as various guests come to the lighthouse to present new mysterious challenges.

At the beginning of each book there is a "Note to Reader." This note encourages readers to use the blank suspect sheets in the back of each book to record the clues they find as they read. At the end of each book, the author gives a follow-up "Note to Reader" before revealing the solution.

The *Mystic Lighthouse Mysteries* can help students use graphic organizers (included in the text), form predictions, and support their conclusions with evidence from the text.

//
Another Exciting Episode: Mystery Series to Explore (cont.)

Mystery Series for Struggling Readers in Grades 4 to 7

***A to Z Mysteries* by Ron Roy**

The Absent Author, The Bald Bandit, and *The Canary Caper* launched this series of beginning chapter book mysteries. Each book focuses on the adventures of Dink Duncan and his friends Josh Pinto and Ruth Rose. The books are written on a second grade reading level and have clear illustrations to assist the reluctant reader.

***Cam Jansen Mysteries* by David A. Adler**

Cam's real name is Jennifer. She has such a photographic memory, however, that her friends have started calling her "The Camera." That nickname has quickly been shortened to Cam. Cam Jansen uses her photographic memory to solve mysteries. The *Cam Jansen Mysteries* are intended for readers ages 7 to 10.

***Jigsaw Jones Mysteries* by James Preller**

Jigsaw Jones and his classmates enjoy solving mysteries. This series is written on approximately a second grade reading level.

Classic Mystery Series for Intermediate Readers

***The Hardy Boys* by Franklin W. Dixon**

Since 1927, the Hardy Boys have been bringing adventures to young readers. There were 58 titles in the original series. Reprints of those original books are available in libraries and bookstores and students still enjoy following Frank and Joe Hardy as they help their father solve crimes.

***Nancy Drew* by Carolyn Keene**

Nancy Drew has never waited for a handsome prince to save her. She has intelligence and courage and she shows readers the power of confidence and integrity.

***The Nancy Drew Notebooks* by Carolyn Keene**

The Nancy Drew Notebooks are written on approximately a second grade reading level and are intended for students who may be too young to read the original Nancy Drew books. *The Nancy Drew Notebooks* follow the adventures of Nancy and her friends Bess and George as third grade students. The mysteries are usually related to school situations and friendship.

Note: Although Franklin W. Dixon and Carolyn Keene are credited as the authors of these series, the books were actually written by a group of authors. Publisher Edward Stratemeyer outlined stories involving his detectives, Nancy Drew and the Hardy Boys, and assigned writers to compose the stories. Carolyn Keene and Franklin W. Dixon did not exist. These names were created by Stratemeyer to unify his group of stories.

The Mystery Series

Another Exciting Episode: Mystery Series to Explore (cont.)

Classic Mystery Series for Intermediate Readers (cont.)

***Trixie Belden* by Julie Campbell**

Fourteen-year-old Trixie Belden loves horses and solving mysteries. She wants to be a detective someday. Trixie and her friends form a club, the Glen-Whites, to solve mysteries and help their neighbors. Originally published from 1948-1986, the books have been enjoying a resurgence since new titles were released in 2004.

***The Boxcar Children* by Gertrude Chandler Warner**

Four children, Henry, Jessie, Violet, and Benny, lived alone in a boxcar after their parents died. These children proved that they could survive on their own. When their grandfather found them living in the boxcar he took them to his large home, offered them shelter, and introduced them to interesting people and places. In each *Boxcar Children* mystery, the four children help their neighbors with good deeds such as saving an animal shelter, volunteering in a local business, and finding lost bicycles. The books stress the values of hard work, honesty, and friendship.

***Encyclopedia Brown* by Donald J. Sobol**

Each volume in the *Encyclopedia Brown* series is a collection of short mystery stories. The reader is challenged to use the clues in the stories to solve the mysteries. Answers to the mysteries appear at the end of each book. Readers often enjoy reading these stories with partners or with a group of classmates. The groups can then discuss the story and work together to find the solution.

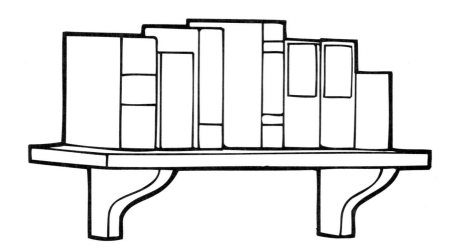

Mysteries Too Good to Miss

The Mysterious Times: Strange Stories of 30 Real-Life Mysteries* by Melissa Heckscher and the Staff of the *Mysterious Times

Published since 1872, *The Mysterious Times* is a periodical which chronicles strange events around the world. This text, *The Mysterious Times: Strange Stories of 30 Real-Life Mysteries*, gives summaries of 30 intriguing cases in a newspaper format. The text contains helpful "Mr. Dictionary" features to explain new terms and boxes containing "Other News of the Day" to help students understand the historical context surrounding the mysterious events presented in the articles.

***Chasing Vermeer* by Blue Balliett**

Stolen artwork, mysterious strangers, and cryptic letters make *Chasing Vermeer* an excellent choice for students who enjoy solving a puzzle. Intriguing illustrations help tell the story of two students who believe that their sixth grade teacher is connected to the disappearance of a valuable painting.

Chasing Vermeer makes many references to the power of the written word and encourages students to think about interesting letters they have written or received. Teachers may wish to use this novel when compiling a thematic unit on forms of communication.

***The Mysteries of Harris Burdick* by Chris Van Allsburg**

This is a fascinating book which encourages students of all ages to write their own mysteries. There is a classroom portfolio edition available with large pictures to display in the classroom.

***Finding Zola* by Marianne Mitchell**

In *Finding Zola*, thirteen-year-old Crystal Ramos solves a mystery while adjusting to life in a wheelchair. Paralyzed in a recent car accident, Crystal shows intelligence, independence, and compassion as she follows clues to save an elderly neighbor.

This mystery offers a compelling plot and subtly teaches respect for the elderly and individuals with disabilities.

***Hoot* by Carl Hiaasen**

Roy Eberhardt has moved from Montana to Florida where even proximity to Disney World can not lift his spirits. Mysterious events occur as Roy rides the bus to middle school and adjusts to new classmates and teachers.

This novel is particularly appropriate for any student who has had to move often and adjust to a new environment.

***Laugh Till You Cry* by Joan Lowery Nixon**

When bomb threats are made to his school, teachers and classmates suspect thirteen year old Cody Carter. Cody must find the true culprit to clear his name and avoid prosecution. *Laugh Till You Cry* offers a fast moving plot with insights into family relationships and middle school adjustments. This is an interesting tale with no violence or inappropriate language.

Mysteries Too Good to Miss (cont.)

The Shakespeare Stealer by Gary Blackwood

The Shakespeare Stealer is an exciting example of historical fiction which can introduce young readers to the Globe Theater and the work of Shakespeare. The main character, fourteen year old Widge, has learned a form of shorthand that enables him to take dictation and copy an entire play as he sits in the audience. Upon learning of his talent, unscrupulous characters order Widge to copy Shakespeare's plays so that the famous playwright's dramas can be performed by rival theater companies.

The references to shorthand make this book an ideal choice for a thematic unit on secret codes.

Skeleton Key by Anthony Horowitz

Fourteen-year-old Alex Rider has reluctantly become a spy for the CIA and he often misses school to solve crimes throughout the world. Alex is the hero of *Skeleton Key*, the third in a series of Alex Rider adventures by British author, Anthony Horowitz. *Skeleton Key* is an extremely fast paced, adventure novel which will keep middle school readers turning the pages.

Who Stole the Wizard of Oz? by Michael Avi-Yonah

Twins Becky and Toby follow clues to find books which have been stolen from the local library. As they search, the students stop to read famous works of childrens' literature and discover the joys of reading.

This is an exciting book for young readers. It offers page turning excitement with no violence or outwardly dangerous acts.

Utterly Me, Clarice Bean by Lauren Child

Clarice Bean keeps a diary in which she describes her adventures at home and at school. When strange events occur, Clarice emulates the ways of her favorite literary detective, Ruby Redfort, and solves the mystery.

Resources for Mystery Lovers

Mystery Writers of America

Mystery Writers of America is a nonprofit organization whose mission is to promote the reading and writing of mysteries by adults and children. This organization sponsors a children's literacy program, *Kids Love a Mystery*, and has designated October as *Kids Love a Mystery* Month. During October teachers are encouraged to invite mystery authors to visit their classrooms to inspire their students with dramatic readings and writing suggestions.

Each year the Mystery Writers of America announce the winners of the Edgar Awards, awards named after famed author Edgar Allan Poe, given to mystery writers in several categories. The *Kids Love a Mystery Reading List* contains the Edgar Award winning and nominated books in the juvenile and young adult categories from 1961 to the present. In addition to recommending mysteries by professional writers, the Mystery Writers of America also encourage students to become mystery writers by promoting the Eddie Award Mystery Writing Program in schools. The organization helps teachers organize writing contests with brochures, certificates, and posters.

Teachers can obtain the *Kids Love a Mystery Reading List,* brochures, posters, and certificates by visiting the Mystery Writers of America website or by using the information below to contact the organization by mail or telephone.

Kids Love a Mystery Website: **http://www.mysterywriters.org/pages/news/klam.htm**

Mystery Writers of America
National Headquarters
17 East 47th Street, 6th Floor
New York, NY 10017
Telephone: 212–888–8171
Fax: 212–888–8107

Resources for Mystery Lovers (cont.)

ReadWriteThink

Teachers can find standards based lesson plans to use with a variety of novels and short stories by visiting the ReadWriteThink website. ReadWriteThink is a partnership between the International Reading Association, the National Council of Teachers of English, and the MarcoPolo Education Foundation. In addition to lesson plans, the website also offers interactive student materials such as a comic book maker and time line makers.

Website: **http://www.readwritethink.org**

International Reading Association
800 Barksdale Road, PO Box 8139
Newark, DE 19714-8139
Telephone: 302-731-1600
Fax: 302-731-1057

Captioned Media Program

A diverse classroom may include students with hearing impairments who can benefit by watching captioned programming. The United States Department of Education offers a federally funded captioned media program which provides free loan of open-captioned videotapes to eligible individuals. These open-captioned tapes can be played on any television/VCR and no special equipment or formatting is needed to show the captions.

Many juvenile and young adult mystery novels are available as videotapes. Teachers can enhance a student's understanding of a mystery novel by showing a captioned videotape version of the novel. Teachers can find open-captioned videotapes by contacting the Captioned Media Program.

Website: **http://www.cfv.org**

Captioned Media Program
National Association of the Deaf
1447 E. Main Street
Spartanburg, SC 29307
Telephone: 864-585-1778 (voice) 864-585-2617 (TTY)
Fax: 864-585-2611

References

McREL Standards. Copyright 2004 McREL, Mid-continent Research for Education and Learning. 2250 S. Parker Road, Suite 500, Aurora, CO 80014

Bear, D.R., Invernizzi, M., Templeton, S., and Johnston, F. *Words Their Way: Word Study for Phonics, Vocabulary, and Spelling Instruction.* Merrill/Prentice Hall, 2000.

Cross, T. Elli. *Essential Roots Word Book.* Educational Tutorial Consortium, Inc., 1990.

Tompkins, Gail E. *Literacy for the 21st Century.* Merrill/Prentice Hall, 2002.

Mystery Texts

Avi-Yonah, Michael. *Who Stole the Wizard of Oz?* Alfred A. Knopf, 1990.

Balliett, Blue. *Chasing Vermeer.* Scholastic Press, 2004.

Base, Graeme. *The Eleventh Hour: A Curious Mystery.* Harry N. Abrams, Inc., 1989.

Blackwood, Gary. *The Shakespeare Stealer.* Scholastic, 1998.

Child, Lauren. *Utterly Me, Clarice Bean.* Candlewick Press, 2003.

Donoughue, Carol. *The Mystery of the Hieroglyphs: The Story of the Rosetta Stone and the Race to Decipher Egyptian Hieroglyphs.* Oxford University Press, 1999.

Doyle, A. Conan. *The Adventures of Sherlock Holmes.* Baronet Books, 1992.

Forbes, Esther. *Johnny Tremain.* Houghton Mifflin, 1943.

Hall, Peg. *Tales of O. Henry: Retold Timeless Classics.* Perfection Learning, 2002.

Heckscher, Melissa & The Staff of *The Mysterious Times.* *The Mysterious Times: Strange Stories of 30 Real-Life Mysteries.* Scholastic, 2004.

Hiaasen, Carl. *Hoot.* Alfred A. Knopf, 2002.

Horowitz, Anthony. *Skeleton Key.* Philomel Books, 2003.

Kehret, Peg. *I'm Not Who You Think I Am.* Dutton Students' Books, 2001.

Lewis, Amanda. *Writing: A Fact and Fun Book.* Addison-Wesley Publishing Company, 1992.

Lowry, Lois. *Number the Stars.* Houghton Mifflin, 1989.

———. *Gathering Blue.* Laurel Leaf, 2002.

Mitchell, Marianne. *Finding Zola.* Boyd Mills Press, 2003.

Nixon, Joan Lowery. *Laugh Till You Cry.* Delacorte Press, 2004.

Petry, Ann. *Tituba of Salem Village.* Harper Collins Publishers, 1991.

References *(cont.)*

Roy, Ron. *The Absent Author.* Random House, 1997.

———. *The Bald Bandit.* Random House, 1997.

———. *The Canary Caper.* Random House, 1998.

Sachar, Louis. *Holes.* Farrar, Straus & Giroux, 1998.

Scieszka, J. *The True Story of the 3 Little Pigs!* Scholastic, Inc., 1991.

Smith, Stan. *Five Minute Mini-Mysteries.* Sterling Publishing Co., Inc., 2003.

Speare, Elizabeth George. *The Witch of Blackbird Pond.* Yearling Books, 1972.

Van Allsburg, C. *The Mysteries of Harris Burdick.* Houghton Mifflin Co., 1984.

Williams, Barbara. *Titanic Crossing.* Dial Books, 1995.

Mystery Series

A to Z Mysteries by Ron Roy

Alex Rider Adventures by Anthony Horowitz

Cam Jansen Mysteries by David A. Adler

Encyclopedia Brown by Donald J. Sobol

Five Minute Mysteries by various authors

Harry Potter by J. K. Rowling

History Mysteries from American Girl by various authors

Jigsaw Jones Mysteries by James Preller

Mystic Lighthouse Mysteries by Laura E. Williams

Nancy Drew by Carolyn Keene

Sammy Keyes Mysteries by Wendelin Van Draanen

The Boxcar Children by Gertrude Chandler Warner

The Hardy Boys by Franklin W. Dixon

The Nancy Drew Notebooks by Carolyn Keene

Trixie Belden by Julie Campbell